T0286949

Cambridge Elements ≡

Elements in the Philosophy of Religion
edited by
Yujin Nagasawa
University of Birmingham

DIVINE HIDDENNESS

Veronika Weidner
Ludwig Maximilian University of Munich

CAMBRIDGE
UNIVERSITY PRESS

University Printing House, Cambridge CB2 8BS, United Kingdom

One Liberty Plaza, 20th Floor, New York, NY 10006, USA

477 Williamstown Road, Port Melbourne, VIC 3207, Australia

314–321, 3rd Floor, Plot 3, Splendor Forum, Jasola District Centre,
New Delhi – 110025, India

79 Anson Road, #06–04/06, Singapore 079906

Cambridge University Press is part of the University of Cambridge.

It furthers the University's mission by disseminating knowledge in the pursuit of
education, learning, and research at the highest international levels of excellence.

www.cambridge.org
Information on this title: www.cambridge.org/9781108711791
DOI: 10.1017/9781108612647

© Veronika Weidner 2021

First published 2021

A catalogue record for this publication is available from the British Library.

ISBN 978-1-108-71179-1 Paperback
ISSN 2399-5165 (online)
ISSN 2515-9763 (print)

Divine Hiddenness

Elements in the Philosophy of Religion

DOI: 10.1017/9781108612647
First published online: April 2021

Veronika Weidner
Ludwig Maximilian University of Munich

Author for correspondence: Veronika Weidner, weidner.veronika@lmu.de

Abstract: This Element introduces the hiddenness argument as presented by John Schellenberg and its up-to-date discussion in a comprehensible way. It concludes with a brief assessment about where things stand, from the author's point of view, and why divine hiddenness should not reduce a reflective theist's confidence in theism.

Keywords: philosophy of religion, arguments against the existence of God, religious epistemology

ISBNs: 9781108711791 (PB), 9781108612647 (OC)
ISSNs: 2399-5165 (online), 2515-9763 (print)

Contents

1 Introduction

The hiddenness of God, as understood by Judaism, Christianity, and Islam, enjoys a rich intellectual and spiritual tradition. Recently, some have argued that the apparent hiddenness of God constitutes evidence for the nonexistence of God. Some proponents of this so-called hiddenness argument suggest that it is as forceful as the argument from evil and shows that theism is unlikely to be true, or is even definitely false. This Element introduces the hiddenness argument as presented by John Schellenberg and its up-to-date discussion in a comprehensible way. In fact, I wish to introduce to you "one of the most dynamic areas in current philosophy of religion" (Green and Stump, 2015, frontmatter).

To begin, I offer a brief account of the hiddenness argument and its main characteristics. I contrast Schellenberg's hiddenness argument, understood as an argument for atheism, with the traditional theistic view that God exists but is hidden. The main part of this Element consists of a clear exposition of the argument's premises, followed by a discussion of the support and criticism other authors have provided for each premise, as well as my own response. Put simply, for each premise I outline Schellenberg's claim as well as what might be said for or against it. This discussion is followed by a short section that considers open questions that may promote further investigation. I then compare the well-known argument from evil with the hiddenness argument. Some of the theodicies and defenses offered in response to the hiddenness argument are similar to responses to the argument from evil, while others are unique to the hiddenness argument, as I demonstrate. In what follows, I sketch some newer types of hiddenness arguments, which are inspired by but go beyond the original argument as developed by Schellenberg. I conclude with a brief assessment about where the debate stands, from my point of view, and whether divine hiddenness should reduce a reflective theist's confidence in theism. Finally, I round off this Element with many references including a dynamic bibliography (in pdf format) by Daniel Howard-Snyder and Adam Green (2017) that I hope students, scholars as well as practitioners will find useful in further understanding and following the debate surrounding divine hiddenness.

2 The Hiddenness of God in the Hiddenness Argument

It is a well-known *theologumenon* that God is hidden. Many theists would not be surprised by the notion that God is hidden when it is first presented to them. In fact, divine hiddenness is such a common antonym or counterterm to the one of divine revelation that theists might not initially be worried about the idea that God is hidden. Of course, the intension and the extension, that is, the meaning and the reference of the term "divine hiddenness" as well as of the term "divine revelation" are understood in various different ways by theists. But it is presumably uncontroversial not just that the meanings of the more general terms "hiddenness" and "revelation" are mutually interdependent (i.e. that the meaning of hiddenness is understood against the background of the meaning of revelation and vice versa) but also that they are reciprocally contrary (i.e. that the meaning of hiddenness is the negation of the meaning of revelation and vice versa). However, regarding the more specific terms divine revelation and divine hiddenness, theists commonly claim that, in the actual world, it is true that God is both hidden and that God is revealed. At an etymological level, the term revelation is derived from the Greek term ἀποκάλυψις or from the Latin term *revelatio*. Both terms signify uncovering something which had been covered or unveiling something which had been veiled (see Dierse et al., 2017).

It will be useful to provide a brief account of the traditional theistic understanding of divine hiddenness. The notion traditionally involved at least two ideas (for more detail on this, see Weidner, 2018: 16–25). The first idea is that God is hidden when a believer, who once experienced the presence of God, loses access to God's presence, sometimes culminating in the painful experience of a dark night of the soul (see San Juan de la Cruz, 1993: 431–487; for commentary on him, see Cockayne, 2018: 73–90, and Coakley, 2015: 233–239). The second idea is that God's hiddenness means that the nature of God is not completely comprehensible to human beings (see, e.g., Rahner, 1975: 285–305, especially 299, 305). At its most extreme, some maintain a view called apophaticism according to which, in its strongest version, God's nature is utterly incomprehensible and ineffable for humans (for a recent account, see Scott and Citron, 2016: 23–49; see also Fakhri, 2020).

God's revelation, in turn, traditionally implies, among other things, that God is available regarding His divine energies (i.e. the effects of God's actions, which are recognizable by human beings). This is what is traditionally called special or supernatural revelation. General or natural revelation, on the other hand, is understood as the idea that all human beings, whether they are believers or not, are able to recognize that God exists by reflecting on certain features of the world or on the fact that there is a world at all (for more on this, see Weidner, 2018: 25–51).

But Schellenberg uses the language of the hiddenness of God or divine hiddenness in a different way. Specifically, he uses it nonliterally. On Schellenberg's usage, these terms do not imply that there is a God about whom something is hidden. Instead, Schellenberg utilizes these terms to refer to the alleged empirical fact that there is or has been at least one human being who, due to no fault of her own, lacks belief that God exists. That is, in Schellenberg's usage, God's hiddenness refers to the observable state of affairs which consists in at least one human being who, through no fault of her own, does not believe that God exists, be it in the presence or past. In Schellenberg's own words, this is what he calls the occurrence of *"nonresistant nonbelief"* (Schellenberg, 2007: 205; see also Schellenberg, 2015a: 17, 74, 75).

So, when Schellenberg claims that the hiddenness of God constitutes evidence of the nonexistence of God, he has in mind this nonliteral understanding of the hiddenness of God. He claims that, on his understanding, proper reflection on what it means to say that God is hidden will lead one to the conclusion that God does not exist. If Schellenberg is correct regarding the nonexistence of God, then, of course, it would be contradictory to uphold the *theologumenon* of the hiddenness of God as it is literally understood by theists (likewise, the revelation of God could no longer be taken literally). That the theistic understanding of the hiddenness of God is self-defeating seems to be Schellenberg's implicit suggestion to theists. Yet, of course, theists will not be genuinely concerned about whether they have been using the term divine hiddenness in the right way. They will worry about whether there is a God, given what Schellenberg has to say in his hiddenness argument.

There is an even more nuanced way of labelling Schellenberg's nonliteral understanding of divine hiddenness. In one of his works, Schellenberg uses the term "propositional hiddenness" (see Schellenberg, 2002: 37). He uses this term because the state of affairs to which he is referring is one in which, at some time, at least one person does not believe the proposition "God exists," due to no fault of her own. Put differently, the truth of this proposition is or was epistemically hidden for that person. This propositional hiddenness can be contrasted with "experiential hiddenness" (see Schellenberg, 2002: 38). The latter term expresses the idea that there is a state of affairs which obtains in the world that contains at least one person who lacks a religious experience of God (i.e. most roughly, an experience in which a person senses the presence of God). Schellenberg's hiddenness argument is prima facie not concerned with experiential hiddenness but seems to postulate only that propositional hiddenness is logically incompatible with the existence of the theistic God. However, upon a closer reading of Schellenberg's defense of the argument, propositional hiddenness is caused by experiential hiddenness. So, the hiddenness argument, in the end, also involves experiential hiddenness.

Let us take a closer look at the specific claims Schellenberg makes in the seven premises of his hiddenness argument. In section 3 (and its subsections) I present Schellenberg's argument and the support for each premise. Additionally, I discuss arguments for and against the truth of each premise. Finally, I highlight further open research questions, thereby aiming to encourage you to come up with even more considerations of your own.

3 The Premises of the Hiddenness Argument

Schellenberg's current hiddenness argument goes something like this:

(1) Necessarily, if God exists, then God is a personal perfect being.

(2) Necessarily, if God is a personal perfect being, then God always loves all human beings perfectly.

(3) Necessarily, if God always loves all human beings perfectly, then God is always open to be in a personal relationship with all those human beings capable of such a relationship with God.

(4) Necessarily, if God is always open to be in a personal relationship with all those human beings capable of such a relationship with God, then God does or omits nothing which would prevent all those human beings to relate to God personally who are capable of a personal relationship with God and also not resistant to a personal relationship with God.

(5) Necessarily, a human being capable of a personal relationship with God who is not resistant to a personal relationship with God is only able to relate to God personally if she believes that God exists.

(6) Necessarily, if God does or omits nothing which would prevent all those human beings to relate to God personally who are capable of a personal relationship with God and also not resistant to a personal relationship with God, then it is not the case that there is a human being capable of a personal relationship with God who is not resistant to a personal relationship with God and yet not able to relate to God personally because she does not believe that God exists.

(7) There is at least one human being capable of a personal relationship with God who is not resistant to a personal relationship with God and yet not able to relate to God personally because she does not believe that God exists.

(8) Therefore, God does not exist. (see Schellenberg, 2015b: 24–25)

This is quite a massive block of text and may seem daunting at first glance. In the following, I will divide it into smaller portions and address each premise in turn. Before that, let's start by noting that the hiddenness argument is a deductive argument (see e.g. Schellenberg, 2015a: 3). The first thing to determine when analyzing an argument in general, and a deductive argument in particular, is whether it is valid or not. That is, does the conclusion necessarily follow from the premises? If yes, then you have a valid deductive argument. If you have a valid deductive argument then, if the premises are true, the conclusion must be true. But, far more interestingly, we still need to determine whether the premises are in fact true. If, for each premise, the answer is yes, then you can deduce that the conclusion is also true. In that case you have learned that you have a sound deductive argument, which is nothing else than a proof. Schellenberg claims that his hiddenness argument is a sound deductive argument against the existence of God, and thus a proof of God's nonexistence (see, e.g., Schellenberg, 2015b: 31). Schellenberg now defends the view that all premises except premise (7) are also necessarily true (Schellenberg, 2015b: 25). However, altering the modal truth status of almost all the premises in this way does not have any effect on the alleged soundness of the argument. This is because, as mentioned, it would suffice that the premises are merely true for the argument to be sound. Neither does the change in the truth status of almost all the premises validly imply that Schellenberg's conclusion must be necessarily true. This would require all the argument's premises to be necessarily true. In what follows, I turn to my discussion of individual premises.

3.1 Premise (1)

(1) Necessarily, if God exists, then God is a personal perfect being.

3.1.1 Background Claims

According to Schellenberg, the hiddenness argument concerns itself with the God of monotheism (or just "theism," on his usage) as found in Judaism, Christianity, and Islam (see Schellenberg, 1993: 10), and "is an argument against the existence of *God* (or against the truth of theism)" (Schellenberg, 2015a: 21). In other words, Schellenberg holds that his argument shows that the God of Judaism, Christianity, and Islam does not exist. But if the God of Judaism, Christianity, and Islam apparently does not exist, it follows that Judaism, Christianity, and Islam are false.

Yet, what sort of being is it that Schellenberg claims is nonexistent? In what follows, I cite from his earliest book and from one of his latest books. First:

> God, if he exists, is *unsurpassably great.* As such, God is to be described (minimally) as ultimate (i.e., the source or ground of all existence other than his own, to whom nothing stands as a ground of existence), personal (that is to say, one of whom agential, intellectual, and affective qualities may appropriately be predicated), and ... all-powerful, all-knowing, perfectly good. (Schellenberg, 1993: 10)

And:

> According to theism, God is a personal creator who intentionally produces or permits everything else that exists ... ; who has all power, all knowledge, and all goodness ... ; and whose love ... makes for our deepest well-being. (Schellenberg, 2019a: 80)

As Schellenberg sees it, Judaism, Christianity, and Islam endorse a concept of God according to which God is unsurpassably great or perfect as well as personal in the sense of being a person. Hence, the theistic God is a perfect personal being (see Schellenberg, 2015a: 90). In other words, the theistic concept of God, as Schellenberg states it, amounts to one which is endorsed by personal perfect being theology. How is it possible to grasp what it means to say that God is a person, according to Schellenberg? All one needs to do is to reflect on what it means to say that a human being is a person and extrapolate this sense of personhood to God (see, e.g., Schellenberg, 2019a: 82).

> God ... [is] a particular being and center of consciousness with power, knowledge, goodness, and love that can be understood by extrapolation from our own similar attributes plus ultimization. (Schellenberg, 2015a: 21)

That is, according to Schellenberg, our understanding of a property ascribed to human beings is a reliable source for our understanding of that property when ascribed to God. The property when ascribed to God must be at least similar to the property when it is ascribed to humans. However, certain properties can be actualized in human beings to varying qualitative degrees. Only the most perfect realization of a human property "could serve as an analogy" of that property as realized in God (Schellenberg, 1993: 18). Schellenberg claims that this practice of extrapolating human properties to understand divine properties is common in theology and philosophy of religion (see Schellenberg, 2002: 45).

Regarding what it means to say that some human is a person, Schellenberg says that it entails that she "can be self-aware and aware of other things, has moral properties, and can act intentionally" (Schellenberg, 2017a: 2; see also Schellenberg, 2019a: 82). Moreover, a person exhibits agential, intellectual, and affective qualities (Schellenberg, 1993: 10). As Schellenberg nonchalantly notes, "I'm assuming we have got our present understanding of a person in view ...; otherwise all bets are off" (Schellenberg, 2015b: 17, fn. 7). And so, according to Schellenberg, when defining God as a person, we should ascribe to God the most perfect realization of the qualities a human person possesses qua "person."

3.1.2 Discussion

Is it true that Jews, Christians, and Muslims all endorse personal perfect being theology? In other words, is it true that their basic theistic claim consists in affirming that God is a personal perfect being, as Schellenberg sees it? According to Schellenberg, the definition of God as a personal perfect being "would ... be accepted by the majority of contemporary theologians and philosophers of religion" (Schellenberg, 1993: 10). In his second book on hiddenness, he affirms this claim again and makes an even broader assertion about who would accept his definition of God, namely, not only the majority of those scholars. Rather, it is a concept of God which is the most popular worldwide among those religious people who affirm that there is any transcendent divinity: "Properly conceived, within a philosophical context, the hiddenness argument will be viewed as a way of testing whether the most common elaboration of ultimism in the world today, the idea of a person-like God ..., can rationally survive" (Schellenberg, 2015a: 21). His claim is that theists in general embrace personal perfect being theology: "[W]hen theists talk about God as a person, they mean that God is the *greatest possible* person. When they say that God exists, they should be taken to mean that the greatest possible person exists" (Schellenberg, 2015a: 95).

However, Schellenberg apparently retracts this view to some degree in a later paper, stating that he has been misunderstood as building his argument against the truth of theism on a commonly accepted concept of God. Here, he clarifies that his concept of God is not necessarily embraced by any theology and that he is aware that there might be other theological concepts of God.

> A philosopher can be thinking about, and hold to be uninstantiated, the idea of a personal God without supposing that what she has in mind has been endorsed by any theology and also without seeing herself as mounting her case against it because it has been thus endorsed. Theologians and their supporters too easily assume – and incorrectly assume, where my argument in particular is concerned – that a philosopher's main aim is to attack theology. ... I fully recognize that the deity I have discussed is not always theology's deity; and so recognizing that what I have had to say about God does not always correspond to what theology has said is merely a small step toward understanding my view rather than the basis for a legitimate criticism of it. (Schellenberg, 2017b: 7–8)

Of course, it would be sensible to reason about God in this way. But if one's argument that God does not exist relies on an uncommon conception of God, then that conclusion will be less significant than if one's argument used a common conception of God. In that case, even if the hiddenness argument is sound, all one would be entitled to conclude is the conditional claim that if theism entails that God is a personal perfect being, then the theistic God does not exist and thus theism is false. But it seems that Schellenberg does not defend a merely conditional conclusion such as this. Rather, he claims that theism entails that God is a personal perfect being, and that, as a conclusion of his hiddenness reasoning, the theistic God does not exist and thus theism is false. In his words, "researchers in *philosophy* should accept that ultimism filled out personalistically (that is to say, theistically) is false because of the case that can be made for the soundness of a hiddenness argument" (Schellenberg, 2015b: 31).

So Schellenberg remains consistent with his previous publications when he repeats the view that the theistic idea of God who is also overall perfect amounts to

> a personal or person-like being who is all-powerful ... and all-knowing, as well as perfectly morally good. ... When this idea of God is the conclusion of an argument, philosophers call the argument an argument for *theism*. Naturally, other philosophers have developed arguments for the denial of theism, the claim that there is no God. When this latter idea is the conclusion of an argument, philosophers call the argument an argument for *atheism*. (Schellenberg, 2019a: 4–5; see also 7–9.13)

Thus, the hiddenness argument is an argument against the truth of theism and thus that a personal God does not exist. That is, in Schellenberg's view the result of testing whether the idea of a personal God and thus theism overall can rationally survive is clear: it cannot. Since the hiddenness argument apparently shows that there is no personal God, atheism is the only way to go. Yet, this has not prompted Schellenberg to leave religion as a topic aside but, instead, to dedicate his subsequent work to carving out other forms of being religious beyond what he considers to be genuinely theistic thoughts (see Schellenberg, 2009, 2013, 2019a, and, especially, 2019b).

> So far we've been largely concerned with how to get here – with properly identifying the road *to* atheism. But having safely arrived, we may wonder, now what? So there's no omni-God. Where can we go from here? The road from atheism I am recommending will take us into further and deeper religious investigation aimed at informing our future cultural life. (Schellenberg, 2019a: 156–157)

Some agree with Schellenberg that Judaism, Christianity, and Islam fundamentally entail personal perfect being theology and that this is a common view. Consider, for example, another Cambridge Element in this series by Natalja Deng in which she states that "'theism' refers to the view that there is a personal God who is omniscient, omnipotent, and omnibenevolent, who created the world, and who is still actively involved in the world. This is intended to capture a core view at the heart of all three Western religions (Judaism, Islam, Christianity)" (Deng, 2019: 3). Likewise, Trent Dougherty asserts that Judeo-Christian and Islamic theism involves at least a concept of God which might be called "*omniGod*" (Dougherty, 2016: 78), that is, a concept of God ascribing omni-attributes like omnipotence, omniscience, and omnibenevolence to God. Hence, according to him, "any argument against an omniGod prima facie counts as arguments against the Abrahamic God" (Dougherty, 2016: 68). This view is also endorsed by Alvin Plantinga (see, e.g., Plantinga, 1974: 165). Richard Swinburne, Schellenberg's former dissertation supervisor at the University of Oxford, describes the God of theism as "a person without a body (i.e. a spirit) who necessarily is eternal, perfectly free, omnipotent, omniscient, perfectly good, and the creator of all things" (Swinburne, 2004: 7).

Yet, some criticize the inherent anthropomorphic inclinations of personal perfect being theology which depict God as "super-duper superman" (see Trakakis, 2015: 194, and the worthwhile literature references he provides by Brian Davies and Fergus Kerr, Paul Helm, and David Burrell who all refuse to see such anthropomorphism as being genuinely theistic, be it in the Catholic Christian tradition, the Protestant Christian tradition, or in any Abrahamic religion). As Michael Rea points out, "[w]ithin a large segment of contemporary Christendom, God has been increasingly portrayed as, in effect, a doting suburban helicopter parent whose entire day is structured around the interests and needs of his or her child" (Rea, 2018: 29).

As Jon McGinnis, a scholar of the Falsafa-tradition, sees it, the concept of God presupposed as theistic in Schellenberg's argument is, in fact, one endorsed only by some contemporary Christian theists. It is not likely to be accepted by medieval Muslim and Jewish philosophers of religion such as Al-Ghazali, Avicenna, or Maimonides.

> [T]he notion of a personal relation presupposes two things: first, an account of person, and, second, the possibility of a relation's holding between two persons. Certain medieval philosophers (and some Jewish ones too) would have found both elements doubtful if not damnable when applied to the purported relation between God and creatures. ... Ironically, then, the atheist who appeals to the argument from divine hiddenness might best be thought of as a "Christian atheist" in as much as he or she apparently agrees more with modern Christians about God than with theists historically and more generally. (McGinnis, 2015: 173–174)

3.1.3 Open Questions

What difference would it make to the significance of the hiddenness argument if the concept of God it assumes is not the only or primary concept of God affirmed by most theists? Is there reason to claim that Christian philosophers of religion and theology too hastily speak on behalf of other theistic traditions without proficiency in these traditions? If so, does this put them in danger of patronization and colonialism in thought, and what might be done to avoid this imbalance or misalignment? What reasons are there for and against a univocal usage of the term "person," whether referring to human beings or God, and are there any sensible alternatives? Would it be possible to personally relate to a God who is not conceived of as a person? Is there reason to think that the analytic approach is characterized by its straightforwardness and striving for clear-cut definitions, and if so, that this may promote a simplified anthropomorphic concept of God who is seen as a mere object of human thought (but not, for example, as that encompassing transcendent and yet immanent reality which is beyond the categories of subject and object but which is the synthesis of subject and object)? Is it plausible to assume that belief in God would not decline as quickly in our Western secular societies if philosophy of religion and theology proposed alternative theistic concepts of God which do not depict God as a perfect human person?

3.2 Premise (2)

(2) Necessarily, if God is a personal perfect being, then God always loves all human beings perfectly.

3.2.1 Background Claims

In the quote cited in section 3.1.1 (Schellenberg, 1993: 10), I have omitted this last qualification of God by Schellenberg.

> As such, God is to be described (minimally) as … perfectly loving. … It might be thought that this is a claim that only Christians have any reason to accept. But I would deny this. … [I]t would seem (and I will assume) that *all* who espouse a form of theism are rationally committed to the truth of the claim that God, if he exists, is perfectly loving. (Schellenberg, 1993: 10–11)

According to Schellenberg, perfect love is not just one property of a personal perfect God among many, but it is one which such a God exhibits necessarily (see, e.g., Schellenberg, 2002: 41) and always (see Schellenberg, 2015b: 20). That is, perfect love is not only some "great-making property" of God (Schellenberg, 2015b: 18), but one of the most central great-making properties of God.

> Without offering anything like a complete explication of "Divine love," I think we can say that what usually goes by that name – at a minimum, self-giving, unconditionally accepting, relationship-seeking love – is such that any being who lacked it would be a being whose greatness *could* be surpassed, and therefore not God. Love of the sort in question is clearly one of the highest manifestations of personal being; so if God is conceived as

embodying the perfections of personal life, he must be conceived as perfectly loving. (Schellenberg, 1993: 10–11)

Schellenberg suggests there is wide agreement among philosophers that "perfect love is an essential property of God" (Schellenberg, 2005a: 201). Initially, he claimed that the recipients of this divine "omni-love" (Schellenberg, 2015a: 96) are, without exception, all human beings (Schellenberg, 1993: 23); the more sophisticated notion of "any finite persons as there may be," which Schellenberg has used more recently (Schellenberg, 2015b: 24), is not taken on here, because there would be no significant difference for his argument. Schellenberg derives the meaning of this omni-love (Schellenberg, 2015a: 95–96) from our understanding of the best love among humans. That is, the most perfect love among humans is the crucial basis for helping us to understand what it means to say that God loves us perfectly. More generally, if a human property is attributed to God, then that property applies to God in a quantitatively and qualitatively amplified way. As previously mentioned, Schellenberg claims that it is

> an intuitively very plausible and widely accepted way of determining the meaning of divine attributes – namely, extrapolation from mundane examples of the relevant properties. ... In other words, what we know of how these terms are used in human contexts provides a prima facie good reason for believing that talk of God is to be understood in the same way. (Schellenberg, 2002: 45–46)

However, despite this allegedly common practice for understanding God's attributes, Schellenberg indicates that this way of determining the meaning of a divine attribute (i.e. by reference to general human experiences and cultural developments) is exactly what characterizes, in his view, a philosophical argument rather than a theological one; theological arguments, instead, rely on revelation for understanding the divine attributes (Schellenberg, 2017b: 7).

3.2.2 Discussion

Is it true that, given God's being a personal perfect being, God would always love all human beings perfectly in the sense suggested by Schellenberg? In discussion of the hiddenness debate up to this point, it has rarely been denied, even by those endorsing classical theism, that perfect love is an essential great-making property of God. There is much more debate about what such divine love implies. While this is further elucidated by Schellenberg in premise (3), some question the adequacy of the method Schellenberg uses to gain an understanding of divine properties such as perfect love. Moreover, some are critical of the univocal use of perfect divine love and love between human beings, for example between a child and a parent, and between a human and

God (see McKim, 2001: 102–103; Ross, 2002: 188; Cuneo, 2013: 160). Rea notes this trend of idealization, saying, "[i]t is widely assumed that divine love is simply an idealized version of one of the best kinds of human love. … God's love is the love of an ideal parent, an ideal spouse, an ideal friend" (Rea, 2018: 63). Yet, as Price argues, if we consider the fact that personal relationships between human beings and God are not relationships between ontological equals, we should recognize that we cannot make an analogy between a personal human–human relationship and a personal divine–human relationship (Price, 1965: 26), not even by idealizing.

3.2.3 Open Questions

Is perfect love a great-making property of God, and, if so, in what respects is this the case, and is it among the most essential great-making properties of God? That is, would God not rightly be viewed as perfectly divine if perfect love were not one of His essential attributes, and why, or why not? What are the influences of cultural evolution on how the best human love is defined, and can we identify any changes in the respective definitions of the best human love, and, if so, in what respects? Would classical perfect being theism also be compatible with the claim that God is perfectly loving; why, or why not? What would characterize an adequate description of God from your viewpoint? If God is described with attributes that can also be ascribed to humans, what is an acceptable method for accurately analyzing the meaning of these divine attributes, and is there any way to verify or falsify our analysis of these attributes? If so, how?

3.3 Premise (3)

(3) Necessarily, if God always loves all human beings perfectly, then God is always open to be in a personal relationship with all those human beings capable of such a relationship with God.

3.3.1 Background Claims

Schellenberg characterizes divine love as "relational-personal love" (Schellenberg, 2007: 199), that is a kind of love that entails "a *pro-relationship* motive, not an anti-bad motive or even a pro-good motive" (Schellenberg, 2017a: 2). This love entails, but also exceeds, mere benevolence toward the beloved. In Schellenberg's view, God's relational-personal love entails that God always seeks a personal relationship with all those human beings who are capable of being in such a relationship with God. And God's seeking relationship at all times entails that God is always open to a personal relationship with all such human beings. In premise (4) Schellenberg addresses the implications of God's openness, at all times, to a personal relationship with all those who are capable. For now, it should be noted that Schellenberg claims that what he says here in premise (3) is a conceptual truth of relational-personal love. That is, the claim that relational-personal love entails that one is always open to a personal relationship with the beloved is deducible merely by reflection on the concept of such love. Moreover, there are empirical instantiations of such relational-personal love, which is the best love to be found among humans, and the best love among humans, as discussed above, is the point of reference for understanding the nature of perfect divine love (see Schellenberg, 1993: 18, and 2002: 46).

Schellenberg argues that God is always open to such relationships with capable human beings because these relationships always have instrumental as well as intrinsic value to God (for further details, see Weidner, 2018: 102–110). They have instrumental value for God because the realization of such a relationship brings about the good of the overall enhanced well-being of the human person involved. And they have intrinsic value for God because such a relationship is a good in itself for God. God's valuing a personal relationship with the beloved for its own sake "is part of what makes the present argument so interesting," according to Schellenberg (2017a: 2). A human being can be considered "capable" of being in personal relationship with God (on the use of the term in premise (3)) if he or she has certain "cognitive and affective equipment" (Schellenberg, 1993: 24) and can thus act on it. That is, such human beings can feel, for example, gratitude toward God or can sense the presence of God. Most humans have the capacity for a personal relationship with God for most of their lives. When a human becomes capable of such a relationship with the Divine, God is immediately open to personal relationship with that human.

A personal relationship is one which is "positively meaningful and reciprocal conscious" (Schellenberg, 2015b: 25). It is called a personal relationship because, first, it is a relationship between two persons (in this case a human person and a divine person), and, second, it possesses the qualities of intimacy and closeness, availability and commitment. Its positive meaningfulness plausibly consists in the fact that this relationship is of significant value for both God and the human involved. Its reciprocity entails that both God and the human involved personally relate to the other in order to know the other person more profoundly (see Schellenberg, 2002: 42). And a personal relationship, as understood by Schellenberg, is conscious insofar as both persons who are involved in it are aware of being personally related to each other. Schellenberg asserts that a personal divine–human relationship may develop over time, go through different stages, and be accompanied by all sorts of different judgments about, for example, its value (see Schellenberg, 1993: 28).

3.3.2 Discussion

Whereas some endorse the whole Schellenbergian concept of what best human love and perfect divine love is, including its implications (see, e.g., Blanchard, 2016: 111), quite a few contest it. Jon McGinnis notes that the concept of divine love and its implications is not compatible with a certain strand of a notable Muslim tradition from the Middle Ages, the Falsafa tradition of Avicenna, a tradition of which Moses Maimonides also approved (see McGinnis, 2015: 157–174). Others have criticized Schellenberg's concept of such divine love as neither a case of eros nor agape, and thus argue that it cannot constitute an adequate concept of love (see Azadegan, 2014: 101–114). Some say that it is at least disputable whether Schellenberg's account of the best human love is a conceptual truth, and thus also whether his account of God's love constitutes a conceptual truth (see also Aijaz and Weidler, 2007: 8). Furthermore, it is objected that Schellenberg presumably says too little, in detail, about what the concept of relational-personal love is. As Keith Yandell puts it, "a discernible ontology of love" is missing here (Yandell, 2012: 211).

Moreover, it seems that there is an inconsistency in Schellenberg's claim that God is only open to personal relationship with those human beings who are capable of a personal relationship with God, even though God's perfect love, as Schellenberg explicitly asserts, extends to all humans, whether they are capable of a personal relationship with God or not (see Weidner, 2018: 98–99). Others, such as Daniel Howard-Snyder, question the truth of the claim that perfect love implies everlasting openness to relationship, because among humans the best human love must not entail such openness (see Howard-Snyder, 2015: 129–130). Consider the following example: your personal relationship with your sister, who has become a heroin addict. She may be emotionally abusive to you and blackmail you to pay for her drugs. In such a case it might be admissible for you to not be open to a relationship with her for a certain period of time. This may be a conscious action motivated by your best conceivable love for your sister, as it may be done precisely for the sake of an even more profound personal relationship with her in the future. In this vein, some put forward reasons why a perfectly loving God might not always be open to some humans. Even if a human is capable of relationship in Schellenberg's sense, as discussed above, some argue that this is not necessarily enough. For it might be that the human has the wrong motives in his or her desire to personally relate to God, and as long as these motives and desires are not changed, God is not open to a personal relationship with her (for a number of such reasons, given in the hiddenness debate, see Howard-Snyder and Green, 2016).

3.3.3 Open Questions

In what respects can it be fruitful and rationally justified to base one's reasoning on brief examples or counterexamples drawn from one's everyday life, as is common in the work of analytic philosophers and theologians? If the concept of love defended by Schellenberg has not been amply clarified, what needs to be added to make it sufficiently complex and adequate, and what might be promising sources for constructing a more adequate account of love? Is it plausible that a perfectly loving God could have a first order desire to be open to personal relationship with humankind, yet have higher order desires that lack such openness to relationship due to a certain state or condition of a human person at a certain time? Might the alleged fact that most human beings are capable of a personal relationship with God for most of their lifetime, as Schellenberg states, be an indicator that there is a God who has equipped those humans with such a capacity when creating them, and if so, what would follow from that? Does affirming that there is a human capability for divine–human relationship, which has been called by some a *sensus divinitatis*, imply the existence of God or not?

3.4 Premise (4)

(4) Necessarily, if God is always open to be in a personal relationship with all those human beings capable of such a relationship with God, then God does or omits nothing which would prevent all those human beings to relate to God personally who are capable of a personal relationship with God and also not resistant to a personal relationship with God.

3.4.1 Background Claims

A God who is always open to personal relationship with capable human persons ensures that all capable humans are able to personally relate to God if they wish to do so. But, as Schellenberg claims, if a human being exhibits resistance toward personally relating to God, then this human being is not able to personally relate to God. Furthermore, in that case there is nothing God can do or omit which would allow that person to freely choose to enter into a personal relationship with God. Schellenberg clarifies that the sort of resistance he is referring to is a self-deceptive resistance toward such a relationship (see Schellenberg, 1993: 27–28). To be a bit more precise, one might read Schellenberg as claiming that such resistance involves (a) a desire not to personally relate to God and (b) actions or omissions supporting her desire not to personally relate to God (see Weidner, 2018: 116). Schellenberg has formerly qualified this nonbelief as being culpable instead of nonresistant, but he now avoids this term because it is liable to be misunderstood (as it has been) (see Schellenberg, 2015a: 54–55). As far as I can see, most authors have not challenged the claim that a lack of resistance toward a personal relationship with God is a necessary (though not on its own sufficient) condition for personally relating to God. Hence, I omit the sub-section "discussion" concerning premise (4).

3.4.2 Open Questions

Consider a specific case in which God is open to personal relationship with a particular human being; does God always personally relate to that human being and offer her the gift of personal relationship with God even if the human being is not able to personally relate to God due to, for example, her resistance toward personal relationship with God? Or does God personally relate to an individual human only if that human personally relates to God? Is there anything God could do to alter a human being's resistance toward God without affecting that person's free will, and if so, what? Does nonresistance involve openness to personal relationship with God, or is lack of resistance simply one of the necessary conditions for having a personal relationship with God, and how could we further understand the difference between openness and lack of resistance?

3.5 Premise (5)

(5) Necessarily, a human being capable of a personal relationship with God who is not resistant to a personal relationship with God is only able to relate to God personally if she believes that God exists.

3.5.1 Background Claims

Even if one is capable of personal relationship with God and nonresistant to such relationship, one must still possess belief that God exists in order to have a personal relationship with God. These are the three necessary conditions which need to be met in order for a human to personally relate to God, according to Schellenberg. While they are each necessary, they are not on their own sufficient but only jointly sufficient. This third condition (i.e. having belief that God exists) is incorporated into what Schellenberg calls his "Not Open principle."

Not Open

Necessarily, if a person A, without having brought about this condition through resistance of personal relationship with a person B, is at some time in a state of nonbelief in relation to the proposition that B exists, *where B at that time knows this and could ensure that A's nonbelief is at that time changed to belief*, then it is not the case that B is open at the time in question to having a personal relationship with A then. (Schellenberg, 2015b: 23)

That is, God would ensure that, as Schellenberg phrases it, the door to a personal relationship with God is never closed to a capable nonresistant believer (see Schellenberg, 2015b: 21). Put the other way around, "the Openness Principle … identifies a *structural* fact about loving behavior that, in the case of God, has the consequence that there will be no reasons, ever, for God not to be open to relationship with those whom God loves" (Schellenberg, 2017a: 8).

As with divine personhood and divine relational-personal love, Schellenberg derives the claim that belief that God exists is necessary for a personal divine–human relationship from what is needed for such a relationship in the merely human context. If a human person lacks belief that the beloved exists, then it is, in Schellenberg's view, not possible for that human person to engage in a personal relationship with the beloved, that is, to communicate with, value, or forgive the beloved.

Furthermore, a reciprocal and conscious relationship between human persons requires that there is another human person to whom one is relating and with whom one is actually aware that one is relating. The same holds for a personal relationship between a human person and God, according to Schellenberg.

> For I cannot love God, be grateful to God, or contemplate God's goodness unless I believe that there *is* a God. … It is important to note that my point here is a logical one. … It is not as though someone who cannot be grateful to God or praise God because she does not believe there is a God could do so if only she *tried* a little harder. Such attitudes and actions are not just contingently difficult but *logically impossible* for one who does not believe that God exists. (Schellenberg, 1993: 30)

Belief in general is defined by Schellenberg as a disposition to think that some proposition is true. So, if someone believes that God exists, Schellenberg claims that this person is disposed to think the proposition "God exists" to be true. Moreover, belief comes in degrees (see, e.g., Schellenberg, 1993: 31–32). That is, someone might exhibit a strong, mediocre, or weak belief. Yet, even weak belief that a person exists is sufficient for someone to personally relate to that person. And the same holds for belief that God exists.

> What all of this would seem to indicate is that we need not concede that belief of a certain (presumably quite high) degree of strength is necessary for personal relationship with God. Even a weak belief that God exists is compatible with gratefulness, love toward God, trust, contemplation, and

the like, for even a weak belief involves a disposition to feel it true that *G*. If I feel, however weakly, that it is true that there is a God, I may be moved to praise him and to struggle with him in prayer. (Schellenberg, 1993: 32)

On Schellenberg's view, belief is involuntary. In other words, no one can choose whether to believe something (i.e. to acquire or sustain a belief); nor can one give up a belief just by one's own will (see Schellenberg,1993: 9–10). But how can one come to believe that a certain proposition is true? What one would need is subjectively sufficient evidence to support the truth of that proposition. Subjectively sufficient evidence is such that, from the perspective of some person, it makes the proposition probably true, so that for her the truth of the proposition is more probable than the truth of the negation of this proposition. Fittingly, Schellenberg also refers to this sort of evidence as probabilifying evidence (see Schellenberg, 1993: 35–38). Regarding the hiddenness argument, Schellenberg asserts that the same holds for belief that God exists. That is, belief that God exists is involuntary and only possible for someone to have if probabilifying evidence is available to her which makes the proposition that God exists for her more probably true than not. According to Schellenberg, God should make such subjectively sufficient evidence for God's existence available to all human beings capable of personal relationship with God (see Schellenberg, 1993: 33) in order to avoid or offset propositional hiddenness as described above.

Schellenberg further holds that there are at least two types of evidence God should provide to everyone: propositional evidence and "experiential evidence" (Schellenberg, 1993: 33). Whereas propositional evidence consists of theistic propositions that may be found in arguments for God's existence, experiential evidence involves a religious experience in which a human person senses the presence of God. As Schellenberg states, "God could give us spiritual receptors and provide a sense of the divine presence" (Schellenberg, 2019a: 101). In defense of his hiddenness argument, Schellenberg focuses on the expected availability of experiential evidence.

3.5.2 Discussion

While many agree with Schellenberg that a human person cannot personally relate to God without believing that God exists, others have developed the view that beliefless attitudes such as hope (see Muyskens, 1979), acceptance (see, e. g., McKaughan, 2013: 109–112), or assumption (see, e.g., Howard-Snyder, 2016: 142–162) might be sufficient for personally relating to God. I have argued for the latter response elsewhere in more detail (see Weidner, 2018: 177–243). It has also been suggested that someone who lacks belief, but exhibits a desire that

God exists and a desire to be in a personal relationship with God, might even come to know God through her openness regarding the idea of God, and, at a minimum, imagine what the fulfillment of her desire that God exists would be like (see Perlmutter, 2016: 51–64). It might be further argued that this human being actually personally relates to God and has a personal relationship with God, which is not unconscious but deliberately sought, even though that individual does not believe that God exists.

This kind of beliefless imaginative faith is something Schellenberg himself proposes in his most recent book (see, e.g., Schellenberg, 2019b: chapter 9), though he does not propose this regarding a deity conceived of as a person. As Adam Green and Eleonore Stump remark,

> [o]ne might wonder, though, whether the belief that God exists is essential to relationship. If there is a kind of faith that does not require belief, one might think that a relationship can grow in the absence of belief. In fact, it could be a great-making feature of a relationship that it grew in a time of uncertainty. (Green and Stump, 2015: 4)

What is more, one might differentiate, as Howard-Snyder proposes, between *de re* awareness of God and *de dicto* awareness of God. He suggests that the former is sufficient for a human to be in a conscious, reciprocal relationship with God "without being aware that God is the one whom she is aware of" (Howard-Snyder, 2015: 138).

Additionally, some argue that Schellenberg expects the theistic God to offer too much: that is, an oversized amount of overwhelming evidence. As Paul K. Moser puts it, we should ask ourselves if we wrongly "expect God to entertain us cognitively, with signs and wonders or with dreams and ecstatic experiences" (Moser, 2002: 121; similarly, see van Inwagen, 2006: 140). But this seems to be a misreading of what Schellenberg claims (see Weidner, 2018: 160–161). Additionally, most of those engaged in analytic debates agree with Schellenberg that belief is involuntary and thus that human persons have no direct control over what they do and do not believe. Yet, Elizabeth Jackson, for example, suggests that "we still clearly have some kind of indirect control over what we believe. We can control our belief-forming habits, what we pay attention to, what we read, who we spend time with, etc." (Jackson, 2016: 99).

3.5.3 Open Questions

If the process of belief formation or suspension is under direct control of the human will, in what respects can God still be held responsible for the fact that some human persons lack belief? Given that God is rightly expected to provide human persons with probabilifying evidence for God's existence but has not done so, is God supposed to violate natural laws in order to provide them with this evidence, and, if yes, how is that idea of divine intervention compatible with the causal cohesion of the world?

3.6 Premise (7)

(7) There is at least one human being capable of a personal relationship with God who is or was not resistant to a personal relationship with God and yet is or was not able to relate to God personally because she does not or did not believe that God exists.

3.6.1 Background Claims

As mentioned above, while Schellenberg claims that premise (7) is an empirical fact in the actual world, it constitutes the only premise which is not claimed to be necessarily true in all possible worlds. This premise states that a certain state of affairs obtains in our world, namely, that there is at least one human person who nonresistantly lacks or lacked belief that there is a God. Schellenberg differs between four types of nonresistant nonbelief, which he claims are all instantiated (see Schellenberg, 2007: 227–228). First, there are *"former believers"* (Schellenberg, 2007: 229) who lost their belief that God exists and would like to regain it. Second, *"lifelong seekers"* (Schellenberg, 2007: 233) are those who never believed that there is a God, even though they have been open to such belief. Third, as a result of their earnest religious search, *"converts to nontheistic religion"* (Schellenberg, 2007: 236) lose their belief that God exists and gain the belief in a nontheistic higher power. Fourth, *"isolated nontheists"* (Schellenberg, 2007: 238) have never had the chance to learn about theism and its claims, so they have never been able to form the belief that the theistic God exists. With regard to this fourth type of nonresistant nonbelief, Schellenberg is referring not only to those communities in our present time who live with no contact with the outside world. He is also relating to a time of *"pre-doubt"* (Schellenberg, 2015a: 79), that is, a time before the formation of world religions such as Judaism, Christianity, and Islam, in which everyone apparently was an isolated nontheist. "And so in the lives of these hunter-gatherers and in their communities, stretching back many millennia before the dawn of recorded history and before anyone ever thought about 'arguments for and against the existence of God,' we find plenty of clear examples of *nonresistant nonbelief*" (Schellenberg, 2015a: 77).

3.6.2 Discussion

Schellenberg is not alone in claiming that premise (7) constitutes an empirical fact in the actual world (see, e.g., Howard-Snyder, 1996: 438; 2006: 354). For example, Howard-Snyder and Green (2016) state: "Schellenberg appeals to increased secularity, especially in Western cultures: what is the probability that *all* of the hundreds of millions of nonbelievers in the secular West are, at the dawn of their capacity to relate personally with God, resistant? Vanishingly small." As Helen de Cruz claims, in the cognitive science of religion (CSR) nonresistant nonbelief is treated as an empirical fact, the occurrence of which needs to be explained. For example, cultural psychological factors are taken into consideration to help understand why there are nonresistant nonbelievers, such as a lack of contact with religious practitioners or the development of national states independent of the churches which have, in part, enhanced the social security, health, and wealth of their populations (Cruz, 2015: 57–58.) There seems to be agreement on this in CSR: "In the picture that CSR offers nonbelief isn't a noetic effect of sin, but a result of our evolutionary history" (Cruz, 2015: 58). Others, however, deny that there is any instance of nonresistant nonbelief in our world, be it in the present or in the past. Hence, in their view, the conclusion that there is no God is a non sequitur from the other premises of the argument (see, e.g., Douglas V. Henry, 2001: 75–92, and 2008: 276–289; also Plantinga, 2000: 184).

Similarly, many doubt that there is a lack of resistance in most (though perhaps not all) instances of nonbelief. That is, they agree that nonbelief occurs in the actual world, yet they claim that much nonbelief is due to resistance toward God (see, e.g., Kvanvig, 2002: 151; Moser, 2002: 147, and 2015: 71–88; Wainwright, 2002: 104; Lehe, 2004: 159, 168–172; Evans, 2006: 241–253; Jackson, 2016: 90–99, 102–105). These accounts of resistant nonbelief frequently appeal to the theological category of sin. Additionally, drawing on results from cognitive science, it has been argued that there is no nonresistant nonbeliever since Schellenberg's account involves an unjustified prediction of the future. That is, contrary to what Schellenberg seems to suggest, it is not clear that if such a nonresistant nonbeliever were to be confronted with probabilifying evidence for the existence of God in the future, then this person would instantly become a believer (see Andrews, 2014: 102–110). And even if this nonresistant nonbeliever were to become a believer, it might still be the case that she may not want to enter into a personal relationship with God, because it seems to be too challenging or eerie.

3.6.3 Open Questions

What further, more specific qualifications of the four types of nonresistant nonbelief as suggested by Schellenberg are conceivable, if any? Does the notion of nonresistance entail that resistance is a genuine option for a human person, and does resistance presuppose that one is familiar with theistic ideas? In which ways might it make sense to characterize resistance as a voluntary or, contra Schellenberg, an involuntary disposition? Why might lack of resistance toward personal relationship with God, rather than openness to a personal relationship with God, be sufficient in order to be able to personally relate to God?

4 Comparisons to the Argument from Evil

Some current questions in the hiddenness debate include the following: whether the argument from hiddenness is as forceful as the argument from evil, and hence whether it should be taken as seriously as the latter; whether the combination of the hiddenness argument and the argument from evil is an obstacle to theism too forceful to rebut; and whether their similarities outweigh their differences. Regarding the latter point, while the details of these arguments differ, it is hard to deny that there are at least five formal characteristics that both arguments share. It is to these similarities that I now turn.

4.1 Formal Characteristics

4.1.1 Anti-Theistic

First of all, the argument from hiddenness and the argument from evil both constitute arguments for the conclusion that the theistic God does not exist. If the claim that the theistic God exists is shown to be false, one need not bother reflecting on the truth of other theistic claims. In this case, theism is bankrupt. But it is important to note that no axiological evaluation is made in these arguments. That is, Schellenberg, in contrast to Thomas Nagel, for example, is neutral on the question of whether it would be a good or a bad thing if God exists. Hence, Schellenberg does not endorse anti-theism, according to which we should not want God to exist (see Kahane, 2011: 674–696; also section 4.2.5).

4.1.2 Modus Tollens

Second, both arguments share the same argumentative structure of *Modus Tollens*. According to this rule of inference, the following holds: (1) $p \rightarrow q$, (2) $\neg q$, and (3) $\therefore \neg p$. That is, both arguments contain a premise that claims that if the God of theism exists (p), then a certain state of affairs obtains (q). In case of the argument from evil, the state of affairs in question consists in a lack of any instance of moral or natural evil, whereas in the case of the hiddenness argument, the state of affairs in question is the nonoccurrence of nonresistant nonbelief. Yet, as both arguments claim, the respective state of affairs does not obtain ($\neg q$). That is, there is at least one instance of moral or natural evil, according to the argument from evil, and there is at least one instance of nonresistant nonbelief according to the hiddenness argument. Hence, these two arguments validly conclude that the God of theism does not exist ($\neg p$).

4.1.3 Logical vs. Evidential Arguments

Third, there are at least two versions of each argument; more specifically, there is a logical and an evidential version of each. Schellenberg now defends his hiddenness argument as a logical argument against God's existence (whereas he earlier defended an evidential version of the argument; see Schellenberg, 1993: 9). That is, on his account the existence of God (if the concept of God is, in his view, understood correctly) is logically incompatible with the empirical fact that there is nonresistant nonbelief. Similarly, the logical argument from evil claims that the existence of God is logically incompatible with the empirical fact that there is moral or natural evil. Recently, Schellenberg has stated that the hiddenness argument "might be said to be an argument from *unrealized good*," since the state of affairs in which everyone who is nonresistant toward God believes that God exists and is thus in a position to personally relate to God is a good state of affairs (Schellenberg, 2018: 189).

An evidential version of the hiddenness argument, in turn, claims that the existence of God is unlikely given the occurrence of nonresistant nonbelief, while an evidential argument from evil claims that the existence of God is unlikely given the empirical fact that there is moral or natural evil. In regard to the argument from evil, some defend an evidential version of this argument according to which it is the amount and kind of evil (i.e. the gratuitous, horrendous quantity and quality of moral or natural evil) which renders the existence of God unlikely. Likewise, an evidential version of the hiddenness argument may be defended by claiming that it is the amount and kind of nonresistant nonbelief (for example, the vast, growing number of nonbelievers who are not only nonresistant toward but very open to and desperately searching a personal relationship with God) which suggests that the existence of God is unlikely to be true.

Although Schellenberg no longer defends an evidential version of the hiddenness argument, others may build on his work and consider defending an evidential version of the argument. One might claim, for example, that some former believers and lifelong seekers may experience suffering, whether consciously or unconsciously, due to their unfulfilled desire to believe that God exists. Furthermore, it might be that a greater number of people would find an argument of this sort, framed as an evidential argument rather than a logical one, plausible. As in the case of the argument from evil, it might be that an argument that renders the existence of God quite improbable might convince more people than an argument that aims at proof of the nonexistence of God (see Anderson, 2019: 87). Objections to these arguments might take the form of either theodicies or defenses. In responding to logical versions of these arguments, one may argue that God's existence is logically compatible with the empirical fact (of evil or hiddenness), and in responding to evidential versions of them one might provide reasons for thinking that the empirical fact is not highly unlikely given that there is a God. A reply is considered a theodicy if one presents reasons God actually has for allowing the empirical fact in question. Alternatively, the reply is considered a defense if one presents reasons God might have for allowing the empirical fact in question, without making the much more epistemically bold claim that these are in fact the reasons God actually has.

4.1.4 Perfect Being Theism

Fourth, both arguments endorse a certain concept of God, namely, they understand God as a perfect personal being. While I have already established that this is an important feature of the hiddenness argument, it is important to note that this is also a feature of arguments from evil. What might follow from that? If God is not conceived of as a personal perfect being exhibiting perfect omnipotence, omniscience, and omnibenevolence, then all an argument from evil may show is that such a personal perfect being does not exist. Yet, it is far from clear that it is warranted to conclude that the God of theism does not exist.

4.1.5 Divine Attributes

Fifth, both arguments focus on one or more of God's essential attributes in arguing that we should expect that the negation of a certain state of affairs ($\neg q$) obtains if God exists. To be more precise, the argument from evil claims that, on the basis of the divine attributes of perfect power, benevolence, and knowledge, we should expect there to be no moral or natural evil in the world. According to the hiddenness argument, we should expect that, given the divine attribute of perfect love, there is no propositional hiddenness in the world. As a result, these arguments specifically deny the existence of a God who essentially possesses the divine attribute or attributes in question. But since God is also stated to possess the divine attribute or attributes in question by necessity, the arguments deny the existence of God in general. However, the divine attributes of concern in these arguments are the divine attributes of God as understood by perfect personal theism.

4.2 Content-Related Characteristics

4.2.1 General Assessments

Schellenberg claims that the occurrence of nonresistant nonbelief and the occurrence of evil are independent from each other and that it is difficult to find similarities between the states of affairs involving the occurrence of propositional hiddenness and evil (see Schellenberg, 2017c: 108–123). Similarly, Peter van Inwagen claims that there is a possible world in which evil occurs but no nonresistant nonbelief occurs and, likewise, that there is a possible world in which nonresistant nonbelief occurs but in which there is no evil (see van Inwagen, 2006: 136–137). In contrast, others defend the view that, given that hiddenness is a bad state of affairs, the problem of hiddenness is a special case of the problem of evil, so that the occurrence of nonresistant nonbelief depends on the occurrence of evil (see Schellenberg, 1993: 6–9; Murray, 1993: 37; Kvanvig, 2002: 159). On the other hand, Dougherty argues that what he calls the existential problem of evil is a special case of the existential problem of hiddenness, so that the occurrence of existential evil depends on the occurrence of existential hiddenness. More precisely, the former problem consists in a human being's experience of an evil state of affairs, whereas the latter problem "is encountered when one either lacks any sense of God's presence or senses his absence," even though the presence of God is expected to be sensed (Dougherty, 2016: 71).

Additionally, Howard-Snyder has argued that the state of affairs in which nonresistant nonbelief occurs is not bad in itself, in contrast to the occurrence of evil; it would only be bad if God actually exists. Moreover, he argues that the fact that there are instances of nonresistant nonbelief in the world constitutes weaker evidence against the existence of God than the fact that there are instances of evil in the world. However, the occurrence of evil in combination with the occurrence of nonresistant nonbelief constitutes much stronger evidence against theism than the occurrence of evil without the latter (see Howard-Snyder, 2006: 352).

4.2.2 Defense vs. Theodicy

Some may question whether God has any sensible reasons for allowing the occurrence of nonresistant nonbelief, even though God is perfectly loving and thus open to personal relationship. As mentioned above, one might develop a theodicy. In a theodicy one offers what one takes to be reasons God actually has for allowing the occurrence of evil or nonresistant nonbelief. More precisely, in a theodicy one argues that some state of affairs that obtains constitutes a good for the sake of which God is willing to permit nonresistant nonbelief or evil. One must then argue that God can instantiate that state of affairs only if God also allows the occurrence of nonresistant nonbelief or evil. In other words, God cannot bring it about that the good in question occurs without permitting that propositional hiddenness or evil occurs.

In a defense, on the other hand, one presents reasons God might have for allowing the occurrence of nonresistant nonbelief or evil. To be more exact, in a defense one argues that a state of affairs that obtains may constitute a good for the sake of which God would be willing to permit the occurrence of nonresistant nonbelief or evil. One then suggests that God can instantiate that state of affairs only if God also allows the occurrence of nonresistant nonbelief or evil. While this is somewhat similar to the case of a theodicy, one need not be sure that the state of affairs constitutes a good such that God is actually willing to allow the nonresistant nonbelief or evil required for its sake. Furthermore, one may consider Luke Teeninga's claim that God possibly allows the occurrence of nonresistant nonbelief in order to permit that a certain state of affairs obtains which constitutes a good in God's eye, if the good in question is significantly better (i.e. more valuable) given that nonresistant nonbelief occurs (see Teeninga, 2017: 589–603).

Several defences and at least one theodicy have been proposed in response to the hiddenness argument as presented by Schellenberg. It is to these defenses and that theodicy that I turn in the next section. I begin by discussing arguments that have been proposed not just as responses to the argument from divine hiddenness, but also as responses to the argument from evil. The goods taken into consideration include unknown goods as well as the good of cognitive and moral freedom, the good of a theistic world, the good of sacrificing one's life for someone, the good of cooperative investigation into whether there is a God or not, and the good of adequate dispositions for a personal relationship with God.

4.2.3 The Unknown Goods Defense

Some argue that it is plausible to think that a good state of affairs obtains for the sake of which God would be willing to permit the occurrence of nonresistant nonbelief, but that we humans are cognitively too restricted to recognize that state of affairs or to recognize that good. One might argue that human beings are either not able to recognize such a good in principle, or that human beings are able to recognize such a good but have not succeeded in recognizing it so far. So-called skeptical theists, such as McKim, propose that there are what he labels "unknown goods of mystery" (McKim, 2001: 87–90, 103). These goods of mystery prompt God to allow the occurrence of nonresistant nonbelief, but they have been and continue to be unknown to us or may even be unknowable for us. But if God can instantiate such a good state of affairs which represents a good for God if and only if God also allows nonresistant nonbelief to occur, then, a skeptical theist might claim, it should not be surprising that the latter is an empirical fact in the world (see also McBrayer and Swenson, 2012: 129–150; Howard-Snyder, 2015: 137–138; for Schellenberg's responses, see, e.g., Schellenberg, 1993: 88–91, and 2005b: 299–301).

4.2.4 Free Will Defense

Cognitive Freedom Defense

Helen de Cruz (see 2015: 58–60) notes that John Hick might have objected to Schellenberg that the good state of affairs for the sake of which God permits nonresistant nonbelief may be that human beings are cognitively autonomous (i.e. free) in relation to God (see Hick, 2009: 133–135). To that end, God might have put human beings at an epistemic distance from God. Furthermore, Hick would argue that being cognitively free regarding God is necessary for being in a position to affirm the truth that God exists (see Hick, 1993: 67, 96). This cognitive freedom is ensured by the ambivalence of the evidence in the world, as it may reasonably be interpreted religiously or not religiously (see Hick, 1993: 67). Furthermore, according to Hick, being cognitively free is necessary for being in a position to personally relate to God. This cognitive freedom is safeguarded by the lack of the overwhelmingly loving presence of God (Hick, 1993: 95–96). But if God's existence and loving presence were obvious to everyone, then human beings would no longer be cognitively free to choose whether to affirm the truth that God exists and respond in love and worship toward God but would instead be coerced to affirm the truth that God exists as well as to love and worship God. As Hick puts it, God has put his creatures at "an epistemic distance, a distance in the dimension of knowledge. They had to be brought into being in a situation in which they are not automatically conscious of God, but in which they have the possibility of freely becoming conscious of him and freely relating themselves to him" (Hick, 1993: 96).

According to Trakakis's reading of Hick's writing, Hick is only claiming that epistemic distance is necessary "for freedom with respect to a personal relationship or commitment to God" (Trakakis, 2007: 217), but not for freedom in regard to belief that God exists or regarding the choice between morally good and bad actions. The important question is whether any interpretation of Hick's defense might make it plausible. Trakakis does not think so. In a critical response to that defense, Trakakis states: "God could have created us in such a way that we accord the proposition that God exists the same self-evident status

accorded to items like '2 + 3 = 5' and 'If a thing is red, then it is coloured'"
(Trakakis, 2007: 222). That is, if every human with suitable intellectual capacities were to acknowledge that the claim that God exists is self-evidently true,
then human beings would still be cognitively free to personally relate to God or
not (see Trakakis, 2007: 222–223).

Moreover, one might wonder whether conclusive evidence in favor of theism
must amount to a proof for God's existence, or whether the awareness of the
loving presence of God must amount to a beatific vision kind of experience on
earth. Instead, perhaps the evidence human beings encounter could merely
make God's existence very probable. And perhaps an encounter with God's
loving presence could be widely available but more subtle and modest, leaving
human beings free regarding whether or not to believe that God exists on the
basis of it, as Schellenberg claims (see Schellenberg, 1993: 95–130, and 2007:
218–226).

Moral Freedom Defense

Second, it has been proposed that the good state of affairs for the sake of which
God may permit nonresistant nonbelief is that human beings are morally free to
choose morally good courses of action or morally wrong courses of action,
thereby allowing them to develop morally significant characters and engage in
their own personal process of soul-making (see Murray, 2002: 62–82, or 1993:
27–38; also Murray and Dudrick, 1995: 109–123). Similarly, others have
claimed that God allows the occurrence of nonresistant nonbelief for the sake
of providing human beings the opportunity to "make a genuine choice of
destiny" (Swinburne, 1979: 211–212). According to this reasoning, if God's
existence, along with the elements necessary for human salvation, were obvious
to everyone, then human beings would be coerced to act in morally good ways
and to refrain from acting in morally bad ways, and they would be deprived of
making a genuine choice of destiny.

Some have argued that the soul-making defense, as proposed by Murray, is
implausible (see, e.g., Lovering, 2004: 89–107). Drawing on narratives which
are both reported in biblical texts as well as based on the way believers act today,
Evan Fales claims that even if the existence of God were evident to human
beings, their cognitive and moral autonomy would still be secured.
Furthermore, it is somewhat likely that more than a few would remain in a
morally bad state in relation to God (see Fales, 2015: 90). As mentioned above,
Schellenberg rejects this kind of free will defense and maintains the claim that if
a perfectly loving God existed, God might create human beings in such a way
that their awareness of God's divine presence, which provides merely

probabilifying evidence for the existence of God, would leave them free to form the belief that God exists and develop morally significant characters.

Others claim that the evaluation of Murray's defense, for example, hinges on the question of what God's plan is for human salvation, which God is supposed to reveal when making his existence evident to human beings, and how that might have an effect on morally autonomous actions. As research in CSR seems to suggest, if God were to reveal Himself primarily as a vengeful, punishing God who threatens that morally wrong deeds will have the consequence, for those humans who commit those deeds, of an eternal afterlife in hell, the moral autonomy of humans would be in danger, and there would likely be an increase in morally good, but coerced, actions. If, however, God were to show himself merely as a loving, merciful God who promises human beings an eternal afterlife in heaven, even in spite of their morally wrong actions, the moral autonomy of humans would not be in danger and a decrease in morally good actions would be likely to occur. As de Cruz states: "Thus, it would be consistent with findings from CSR that God could reveal some aspects of himself (e.g., being loving) while keeping other elements hidden, without compromising our ability to make moral choices" (Cruz, 2015: 60).

4.2.5 The Pro-Theism Defense

A new question under debate in analytic philosophy of religion and theology is whether or not the existence of God, and thus the truth of theism, might be a good or a bad thing. More specifically, would the existence of God add value to the world, and thus count as a good in the world, or not? Some argue that a theistic world (i.e. a world in which God exists) which, like ours, contains nonbelief, would be significantly better than an atheistic world. This is because such a theistic world would include not just what we might call "theistic goods" (such as cosmic justice or an eternal afterlife for human beings) but it might also actually allow for at least the experience of atheistic goods such as "privacy, independence, autonomy, and certain types of dignity" (Lougheed, 2018: 332). According to this argument, the experience of any given good x is, in axiological terms, as valuable as the actual obtaining of x.

An objection to this defense is that it is implausible to claim that it is possible to experience certain atheistic goods, such as the experience of privacy, in a theistic world because having an experience of a good such as privacy requires that the good in question actually obtains. The reason for this, as Hendricks and Lougheed argue, is that "experience" is a success term (i.e. a term which is correctly used only if the state of affairs it describes does, in fact, occur). Therefore, a theistic world in which the existence of God is not evident to everyone would not rightly be regarded as more valuable than an atheistic world. This objection also proposes that an atheistic world, in turn, would not only include the experience of atheistic goods, but might also include the experience of theistic goods, even though God does not exist. Some of the theistic goods that might be experienced in such an atheistic world include near-death experiences, cosmic justice, divine intervention, and even personal relationship with God (see Hendricks and Lougheed, 2019: 6–15).

4.2.6 The Self-Sacrificing Love Theodicy

Andrew Cullison argues that the good state of affairs for the sake of which God permits propositional hiddenness in the actual world is that the greatest and most noble goods can be attained by some when they lay down their lives, as a true sacrifice of love, so that others may live. Perhaps this line from the bible comes to mind when reading this: "No one has greater love than this, to lay down one's life for one's friends" (John 15:13). To choose to die so that another person may live is commonly considered a supererogatory act (i.e. a morally praiseworthy act beyond what is morally obligatory). Cullison is not claiming that the good of being able to perform this supererogatory act could not be attained and evaluated as a noble act if propositional hiddenness did not occur. He distinguishes between different qualifications of this good. According to Cullison, "a really great and noble good" (Cullison, 2010: 127) is attained only if, in a world in which the existence of God is not obvious to everyone, a metaphysical naturalist (i.e., very roughly, someone who believes that there is no supernatural deity or reality) sacrifices her life for someone else. In fact, it is a much greater and more noble good than the merely noble good attained if a "*psychologically certain* theist" (Cullison, 2010: 128) sacrificed her life for someone else. Furthermore, Cullison claims that, given the occurrence of propositional hiddenness, only if a naturalist lays down her life for somebody does this "count as a *genuine sacrifice*" (Cullison, 2010: 129).

Drawing on considerations by Eric Wielenberg (2005: 91–92), Cullison's background assumption is that, in a world in which it is not obvious that God exists, a naturalist "woman who sacrifices her life to save her child may well have accepted a fate worse than the one she deserves, and in so doing she may have spared her child a fate worse than the one it deserves" (Wielenberg, 2005: 92). That is, the woman who does not believe that there is a God who is "a divine guarantee of perfect justice" (Wielenberg, 2005: 91), rewards morally praiseworthy actions, and grants an eternal life after death accepts a worse fate than she deserves in terms of a premature end of her life and spares her child a worse fate than it deserves in terms of a premature end of its life. "Only without God is this highest form of self-sacrifice, one of the most admirable kinds of human action, an available option" (Wielenberg, 2005: 92).

4.2.7 The Cooperative Investigation Defense

Others have argued that the good state of affairs for the sake of which God might permit nonresistant nonbelief is that human beings can, and actually do, investigate important questions about the existence and nature of God together, and that they support each other in that endeavor (see Swinburne, 1998: 211–212; McKim, 2001: 81–82, 103). Furthermore, those who have come to affirm the truth of God's existence are thus able to help others to do likewise, so that human beings thereby take deep responsibility for each other in such existential matters (see Swinburne, 2004: 222–228; Dumsday, 2010: 357–371; Crummett, 2015: 45–62).

Schellenberg objects to this defense, claiming that this collective endeavor may be possible even if God's existence were more evident (see Schellenberg, 1993: 191–199). Additionally, it might be argued, drawing on considerations from social epistemology, that the failure of such endeavours, and the miscommunication of theistic evidence by theists to nontheists on an interpersonal, informal social, and institutional level, actually shows that human beings do not take deep responsibility for each other, and may even be causing further nonresistant nonbelief to arise (see Greco, 2015: 109–125).

4.2.8 The Good Disposition Defense

Some argue that the good state of affairs for the sake of which God may allow nonresistant nonbelief to occur is that human beings can consciously become willingly well-disposed toward a personal relationship with God. They argue that actual nonresistant nonbelievers might either not be well-disposed to personally relate to God at present (see McKim, 2001: 100–101; Lehe, 2004: 161–167), or they may be well-disposed but need to become aware of and voluntarily affirm their good disposition and develop the proper motives for a personal relationship with God (see Howard-Snyder, 1996: 440–453, and 2015: 132–137; Moser, 2002: 120–148, and 2008: 105–113; Tucker, 2008: 269–287; Dumsday, 2014: 193–207).

Schellenberg rejects both strands of thought (regarding the former, see Schellenberg, 2005b: 296–298; regarding the latter, see Schellenberg, 2008: 289–293). More generally, according to Schellenberg, God might permit the occurrence of what he calls a "secondary sort of hiddenness." That is, Schellenberg suggests that God may temporarily withdraw from the believer, as understood in the *theologumenon* of the dark night of the soul, which would not result in loss of belief but would allow human beings to develop positive dispositions toward personal relationship with God (see Schellenberg, 1993: 203–204, or 2005b: 299–300).

4.2.9 A Bunch of Defenses

Howard-Snyder and Green seem to be right when they state that

> it's doubtful that any single one of them [i.e. these defenses] offers a total explanation of nonresistant nonbelief. Different kinds of nonresistant non-believers, given the rest of their psychology, might call for different expla-nations. Moreover, each of these explanations, taken alone, might fail to provide a total explanation of any particular kind or instance of nonresistant nonbelief, and yet each of them might provide a partial explanation and, taken together with others, add up to a total explanation. ... Thus, if we are to reject these explanations, and others that might be proffered, we must claim that they fail, collectively as well as individually, to account for why God might permit nonresistant nonbelief. (Howard-Snyder and Green, 2016)

Furthermore, it should be noted that God, if God exists, "might have different reasons for the same individual at different times" (Howard-Snyder, 2006: 355).

Schellenberg's response to all greater-good defenses consists in defending what he calls an "'accommodationist' strategy" (Schellenberg, 2005b: 287). In other words, Schellenberg claims that all good states of affairs that have been proposed or might be proposed in greater-good defenses could also be accom-modated within a divine–human relationship. As a result, no such defense is successful in offering a reason why God might allow nonresistant nonbelief to occur (see, e.g., Schellenberg, 2005b: 299).

5 Other Types of Hiddenness Arguments

In this section of the Element I present other hiddenness arguments, which are inspired by but go beyond the original argument proposed by Schellenberg.

5.1 The Nonbelief of Gospel Message Argument

As Theodore Drange states, Schellenberg's hiddenness reasoning "is directed only at the problem of nonbelief in God's existence, not the quite separate problem of nonbelief in the gospel message" (Drange, 1998: 62). Yet, according to Drange, the fact that there have been many lifelong nonbelievers in respect to all the propositions of the gospel message in the time after Christ constitutes evidence against the truth of evangelical Christian theism. As Drange points out, the central propositions of the gospel message in the Christian New

Testament include, *inter alia*, God's incarnation in Jesus Christ and the latter's death and resurrection, as well as redemption of humankind. If the God of evangelical Christianity exists, it should not be expected, according to Evangelicalism itself, that there have been many lifelong nonbelievers who lack belief in respect of the whole gospel message in the time after Christ. On the contrary, it should be expected that, in the time after Christ, the majority or totality of human beings start to believe in this gospel message at some point in their individual lives, if the God of evangelical Christianity exists. But, "it is *not* the case that all, or almost all, humans since the time of Jesus of Nazareth have come to believe all the propositions of the gospel message by the time of their physical death" (Drange, 1998: 60; see also Drange, 1993: 417–432).

Hence, Drange concludes that the God of evangelical Christianity does not exist.

5.2 The Demographics of Nonbelief Argument

Maitzen builds an additional hiddenness argument according to which it is the vast amount, and geographically uneven distribution, of nonresistant nonbelievers throughout the world which constitutes evidence against the truth of theism. Maitzen claims that there are some places in the world where only a very small percentage of people believe that the God of theism exists, whereas the vast majority of people in those places believe something else, such as that the Hindu deity Vishnu exists. On the other hand, there are other places in the world where it is the other way around – the vast majority believe that the God of theism exists and only a small percentage of the population believe that Vishnu exists. According to Maitzen, if the God of theism does not exist, then such demographics of nonbelief are to be expected and are easily explainable. This is because, as Maitzen argues, if this were the case then it would only be sociocultural, historic, or geographic contingencies that determine whether human beings have belief or lack belief that the God of theism exists. "Theistic explanations must account for this geographic patchiness in terms of reasons God might have for allowing it, and such reasons seem hard to find" (Maitzen, 2006: 183).

On Maitzen's view, metaphysically naturalistic accounts can better explain the fact of the vast number and geographically uneven distribution of nonresistant nonbelievers. Even if there may be convincing reasons for thinking God would allow the occurrence of nonresistant nonbelief in an individual, these reasons fail to explain why God would allow the uneven distribution of nonresistant nonbelief throughout the world. That is, these reasons might only provide a satisfactory explanation of nonresistant nonbelief if its occurrence were distributed evenly throughout the world. Furthermore, some of the proposed explanations of the occurrence of nonresistant nonbelief, such as the aforementioned Good Disposition Defense (see section 4.2.8), are not likely to be successful when we take into account the uneven demographics of nonbelief. For these dispositions "do not cluster by country or culture so as to show up twenty times more often in Thailand than in Saudi Arabia" (Maitzen 2006: 184).

Perhaps, in order to respond to Maitzen's account, there needs to be a sort of meta-defense which elucidates why God might allow that these explanations for the occurrence of nonresistant nonbelief do not apply to every region in the world. That is, it may be argued, there needs to be a meta-defense which makes a plausible case that the goods for which God is claimed to be willing to allow nonresistant nonbelief are instantiated in certain regions of the world more than in others. Jason Marsh has objected to Maitzen's anti-theistic argument. If Molinism is true, he argues, and God thus has middle knowledge, God knows in advance that some human persons would not freely believe in God unless they encountered a beatific vision of God. Hence, God waits, making God's existence evident to these persons only after the end of their earthly life, in order to allow them to be saved eternally (see Marsh, 2008: 465– 471; for Maitzen's response to Marsh, see Maitzen, 2008: 473–477). Timothy Mawson replies to Maitzen that, if Calvinism is true, God pre-elected some human beings for heaven as their final destination, and these persons are those who turn out to believe that God exists during their lifetime. Those, however, who nonresistantly lack belief that God exists are those who God chose in advance to end up in hell (see Mawson, 2012: 184–204). Moreover, Max Baker-Hytch claims that the demographics of nonbelief is a state of affairs which may be expected whether or not God exists, so that, on its own, it does not constitute an objection against theism. Given mutual epistemic dependence (i.e. the fact that human persons rely on the testimony of their own social contexts for their beliefs), this uneven distribution of belief and nonbelief is to be expected. Since such mutual epistemic dependence supports the realization of goods such as reciprocal trust, the avoidance of (self-)deception, and mutual help in the process of epistemic understanding, God has good reason to allow for mutual epistemic dependence and thus for the uneven distribution of belief and nonresistant nonbelief (see Baker-Hytch, 2016: 375–394).

5.3 The Natural Nonbelief Argument

Marsh provides an argument that focuses on the fourth category of nonresistant nonbeliever mentioned in section 3.6.1: isolated nontheists. He argues that the fact that, for most of human history, everyone was an isolated nontheist, constitutes evidence against the truth of theism. That is, if the God of theism existed, Marsh argues, then it is highly unlikely there would have been such a long time in the history of humankind in which it was natural for everyone to lack belief that there is a God. As Marsh claims, "early humans … originally lacked a concept of God and were religiously restricted to concepts of limited … supernatural agents. As a result, many early humans … failed to believe in God … The nonbelief in question was both naturally occurring and nonresistant" (Marsh, 2013: 359). Why would the God of theism, if that God existed, not have done anything about this? On the other hand, Marsh argues that a lengthy period during which the world contained only natural nonbelievers would be highly likely, according to the view that people evolved via natural selection and random mutation (Marsh, 2013: 361). In other words, according to Marsh, metaphysical naturalism offers a better explanation than theism for the vast time span when there were only natural nonresistant nonbelievers.

In a critical response to Marsh, Kevin Vandergriff argues that this occurrence of natural nonbelief is not evidence against the truth of theism. As Vandergriff sees it, there might be a morally sufficient reason why God allowed natural nonbelief to occur among early humans. The reason is that God might have an axiarchic goal for reality which consists in God's aiming at the realization of "a choiceworthy degree of moral, intellectual, and aesthetic value" (Vandergriff, 2016: 36) in the world in general and for human beings in particular. Vandergriff claims that this view, called Axiarchism, is commonly agreed to be entailed by theism. According to Axiarchism, God allows the occurrence of a state of affairs insofar it adds to the moral or aesthetic value of the world overall. "This implies that for any human person X, God will providentially place X in circumstances which best promote a life of choiceworthy meaning for X in this life and the next" (Vandergriff, 2016: 37). But the realization of such value is probably possible only if God allows that natural nonbelief occurs, and especially so in the early history of humankind, as Vandergriff claims.

6 A Brief Assessment

So far, I have presented the many-sided, ever-evolving challenge of atheistic hiddenness reasoning and the wide disagreement about whether this reasoning is plausible. In this final section, I sketch where the debate stands from my point of view. Does the hiddenness argument by Schellenberg at least minimally succeed in lowering confidence in theism? I do not think so, for two reasons. The first reason is that the argument is based on some claims whose truth is more than questionable. But, if at least one premise is not true, then the conclusion cannot be true either. The second reason is that there are some promising defenses which together provide a plausible explanation as to why God might allow propositional hiddenness to occur. As a result, neither a logical version of the hiddenness argument (i.e. one that supposes that the occurrence of propositional hiddenness is logically incompatible with the existence of God) nor an evidential version of that argument (i.e. one that supposes that the occurrence of propositional hiddenness renders the existence of God to be unlikely) has great prospects of success. That said, the hiddenness argument not only deserves full attention for the legitimate queries it raises regarding the truth of theism. Schellenberg also needs to be acknowledged for unintentionally elucidating the shortcomings of some claims which are generally common in contemporary analytic debates. It is these shortcomings which, I hope, will in turn encourage further inquiry into the compelling themes with which they are concerned. Furthermore, the debate about the hiddenness of God nonliterally understood may help us see again the importance of the *theologumenon* of the second aspect of God's hiddenness, literally understood, as mentioned in section 2, that is, the incomprehensibility of God's nature.

6.1 Personal Perfect Being Theism Is Not the Only Option

To begin, which are the claims of the hiddenness argument the truth of which I view as more than questionable? In response to premise (1) (see section 3.1), I disagree with Schellenberg that Jews, Christians, and Muslims all endorse personal perfect being theology. In other words, I object that their basic theistic claim consists in affirming that God is a personal perfect being. Of course, I agree that personal perfect being theology has been influential in the traditions of Judaism, Christianity, and Islam. What is more, I recognize that this is the prevalently used concept of God in the current analytic debate, as the quote by Deng in section 3.1.2, for example, illustrates.

What, nowadays, counts as analytic philosophy of religion or analytic theology is best understood as a shared commitment to a certain method or style of argumentation rather than any agreement on the content of philosophical or religious claims. Yet, most of these scholars are at least influenced by one of the religious communities of the various Christian denominations (such as Catholicism, Lutheranism, or Russian Orthodoxy), whereas those from a Jewish or Muslim background are, unfortunately, still underrepresented. That is, this scholarly group of analytics predominantly consists of those who either identify as theistic Christians engaged in one of the diverse denominations of Christianity, or whose agnosticism or atheism is, at least implicitly, directed at Christianity. As I see it, it is no wonder that Schellenberg claims that it is uncontroversial that the theistic concept of God consists in viewing God as a personal perfect being, and even describes Saint Paul the Apostle as a personal perfect being theologian (see Schellenberg, 2019a: 77). For from the founding days of (metaphysically friendly) analytic philosophy of religion in the later second half of the twentieth century, Plantinga and Swinburne began to portray God as a personal perfect being with these omni-attributes, and most analytical scholars followed them in this regard. And since that definition of God is so often cited and used in analytic debates, it is understandable to suppose that, even within the larger context of history, personal perfect being theology is generally the best point of reference when conceptualizing God.

Yujin Nagasawa rightly points out that "[p]erfect being theism is arguably the most widely accepted form of traditional monotheism. It has been the central notion in the philosophy of religion over the last few centuries and it has always been the focus of philosophers of religion when they address the existence and nature of God" (Nagasawa, 2017: 7). But a survey of historic as well as contemporary writings reveals that there are at least two kinds of perfect being theology: classical perfect being theology and personal perfect being theology. It is far from clear that only the latter, as entertained in current analytic writing, constitutes the core of theism. As Thomas Schärtl points out, the former entails what Brian Davies calls classical theism, whereas the latter includes, in Davies's terminology, personal theism (see Davies, 2004: 9–11, and Schärtl, 2016: 27). Schärtl suggests that personal theism is what he calls the offspring of classical theism, which presumably originated during the time of the Enlightenment. Therefore, it is a younger view than classical theism in the course of intellectual history (see Schärtl, 2016: 3,28). But if the view that God is a personal perfect being is not the primary claim shared by all elaborations of theism, then the hiddenness argument (even if otherwise sound) does not prove that the God of theism does not exist, and thus it does not prove that theism is false. What the hiddenness argument may show (again, if otherwise sound), is that a divine personal perfect being does not exist and thus theism understood as personal perfect being theology is false.

Perfect being theology, which classical theism and personal theism have in common, pictures "God as the most perfect, ontologically and morally superior, even all-surpassing entity" (Schärtl, 2016: 27). But how do classical theism and personal theism differ? As Davies illustrates, according to classical theism God is eternal and simple, characterized by immutability and impassability (Davies, 2004: 5–9). Moreover, classical theists stress God's unknowability and unrecognizability, that is, the hiddenness of God's nature literally understood (as sketched at the beginning of this section; see Schärtl, 2016: 26–27). Classical theism has stressed the transcendence and thus ineffability of God (see Rea, 2015: 210–225). Highlighting the most fundamental

Otherness of the Divine, apophatic voices warn against the illusion that God is an object of thought, like any other object of thought, who is utterly knowable and easily describable. I do not wish to propose a fully fledged negative theology here, which risks silencing any discourse about religious matters. Yet, I admit to valuing the fact that classical theists seem to take more seriously the metaphysical status of that transcendent Divinity we are trying to conceptualize with our limited human minds. I have increasingly come to understand the caution of these theists against anthropomorphic, univocal speech about God.

Anselm of Canterbury is often referred to as the initiator of perfect being theology, even though perfect being theology was presumably introduced before the days of Anselm (see Nagasawa, 2017: 24). According to Anselm's famous formulation, God is "aliquid quo nihil maius cogitari possit" (Anselm of Canterbury, 1968: II, 5), that is, that than which nothing greater can be conceived of. Schellenberg explicitly grounds his view of what he takes to be the fundamental theistic concept of God in Anselm's writings (see Schellenberg, 2019a: 142–143). Yet, as Schärtl elucidates regarding Anselm and the later medieval tradition, it is highly questionable that "[p]ersonhood in God is fundamental for traditional theists" (Schellenberg, 2019a: 148). As Schärtl (2016: 7) states: "Attributes indicative of personality and personhood seem to play a rather minor and subordinate role in the Anselmian concept of God, as compared to those of spirit and substance."

Likewise, theists in the whole medieval tradition did not primarily conceive of God as a person, literally understood.

> Using the words of the classic medieval doctrine, God is *a perfect, eternal and unchangeable "substance"*. ... Admittedly, medieval theologians and philosophers were eager to underline that God, who is being in itself in the most perfect and unrestricted way, is also *worthy of worship, devotion and love*. But what the medieval tradition had to say about divine knowledge, intention and will, as well as divine agency and providence, is not obviously compatible with the everyday concept of a person. For how should we reconcile the idea that, on the one hand, the primary object of God's knowledge and will is the divine nature and that divine agency must be conceptualized as one, eternal act while, on the other hand, the notion of personhood revolves around distinct stages of consciousness, the prospect of having access to external objects or the displaying of a variety of intentions and emotions alongside distinct temporal sequences? ... "[R]eal classical theism" gives sufficient reason to criticize the very idea of a personal God to begin with – by emphasizing divine substantiality, aseity, simplicity and eternity, in contrast to what some thinkers nowadays take to be the essential attributes of the divine nature. Thus for Avicenna and St. Anselm to abandon the idea of divine eternity, aseity and necessity would amount to abandoning the belief in God as such. So if we can agree that Avicenna or St. Anselm represent a

paradigm of classical theism, then classical theism is by no means guilty of nurturing an anthropomorphic concept of God. (Schärtl, 2016: 7,14)

In agreement, Andrei A. Buckareff and Yujin Nagasawa reference John Bishop in stating the following:

> That God is personal or a person according to what might be properly labeled as "classical theism" is controversial. If the progenitors of classical theism are taken to be the likes of Anselm, Ibn Rushd, Maimonides, and Thomas Aquinas, then it is not clear that they literally took God to be a person. They all recognized a point to anthropomorphic language while remaining hostile to taking any such representations of God literally. (Buckareff and Nagasawa, 2016: 1, fn. 1)

Personal theism, on the other hand, which endorses personal perfect being theology, affirms that the Divine is "a personal God who is regarded as a conscious, wise, morally praiseworthy, and bodiless individual which has enormous powers and capacities at his disposal" (Schärtl, 2016: 6). I fear that such a personalized concept of God risks an anthropomorphic understanding of God which is also criticized within analytic philosophy of religion (see above the quotes by Trakakis, 2015, and Rea, 2018, in section 3.1.2). It is a natural step to then use the term "person" as well as, for example, "love" univocally in regard to both human beings and God. Yet, Thomas Aquinas had already dismissed univocal speech as not adequate when it comes to making statements about God (see Thomas Aquinas, 1952: I, *q.* 13, *art.* 5). What is more, Schellenberg's univocal application of personhood to both humans and God overlooks the controversy over what constitutes personhood even in the human case. That is, the philosophical debate about human personhood has not clearly resulted in any widely agreed upon conclusions. For example, the question of whether empirical functionalism or ontological personalism is true (i.e. whether a person is defined by exhibiting some functions or abilities, or by virtue of her ontological status as a finite being) is never addressed in Schellenberg's argument.

Hence, I accept the following assessment from Rea, albeit without restricting the target of Schellenberg's use of this concept of God to American evangelicalism, but to the majority of those international scholars engaged in analytic debates – whether they are influenced by or engaged in any religious community such as Catholicism or Greek Orthodoxy.

> Even if the Schellenberg problem fails as an argument against the existence of the God of theism in general, or as an argument against the existence of the God of traditional Christian theism in particular, it still poses a threat to belief in a God about whom Schellenberg's theological assumptions are true. Many

theists do accept those assumptions; so although it is an attack on a straw deity if the God whose existence it targets is supposed to be the God of theism or of traditional Christianity, the Schellenberg problem can easily be reframed as an argument with a real, definite target. I suspect that Schellenberg's God has some claim to being the God of certain strands of contemporary American evangelicalism. (Rea, 2015: 224–225)

In addition to this older form of perfect being theology maintained by classical theists, there is a novel form of perfect being theology proposed by Nagasawa as another alternative to personal, omni-God theism. Nagasawa defends what he calls a maximal-God theism, that is, theism which entails a concept of God as a maximally great being or as "the being that has the maximal consistent set of knowledge, power, and benevolence. The maximal God thesis suggests that, while God is certainly very knowledgeable, very powerful, and very benevolent, He might or might not be omniscient, omnipotent, and omnibenevolent" (Nagasawa, 2017: 92). If Nagasawa is correct, then the hiddenness argument is not successful in showing that perfect being theism is false overall; at best, it shows that personal perfect being theism is erroneous. And, certainly, if classical theism is a viable form of theism, then the hiddenness argument is likewise not a convincing refutation of theism as such.

As we have seen, it is a specific (i.e. personal) theistic concept of God that Schellenberg employs. However, as noted above, it is important to stress that personal perfect being theology, for many analytic philosophers of religion, whether they are theistic, atheistic, or agnostic about theism, is the assumed understanding of God. So Schellenberg does not stipulate this as his view in a random fashion, but simply takes seriously what many in the analytic debates on topics within philosophy of religion take to be their understanding of God. Schellenberg has since concluded that, even though this personalized perfect being called God apparently does not exist, some other nonpersonal transcendent reality might exist. This has motivated him to continue exploring religious questions in the context of what he calls evolutionary religion. But if there are alternatives to personal perfect being theology within theism (e.g. classical perfect being theology), which constitute "*any elaboration* [of ultimism] *that doesn't make the personal that fundamental*" (Schellenberg, 2019a: 170), perhaps Schellenberg might sympathize with theism again.

6.2 Divine Attributes Are Not Humanlike Perfections

In my view, it is problematic to merely extrapolate from our understanding of human personhood in order to understand divine personhood, or from best human love to divine love – as in premises (1) and (2) in section 3. There might not be any viable alternative methods, though, you may object, a conceptual construct developed by a human being plausibly refers to and is limited by what a human being can experience, reflect upon, and imagine. Of course, I agree that we are limited by and restricted to our finite intellectual mindset. Yet, the danger of overly anthropomorphizing God in personal theistic accounts consists in supposing that the similarities between, for example, best human love and perfect divine love prevail over their dissimilarities. As a result, one tends to a univocal use of the terms, for example, of perfect divine love and the best conceivable love between human beings and all too easily stipulates some claim about ideal love as a conceptual truth (i.e., more precisely, the propositional content of the term "ideal love" as logically–conceptually true) which might, in fact, be erroneous.

I would regard it as worthwhile to take a second look at the terms love and personhood and whether what they refer to and mean is so uncontroversial. In doing so, it might also be helpful to differentiate whether, for example, a human being's openness to personal relationship is rightly seen as a first-order desire or as a second- (or higher-) order desire. For instance, concerning love, one could look at some writings that provide a deep analysis of the nature of love (see, e.g., Fromm, 1956; May, 1969; or Oord, 2010). What is more, being aware that the dissimilarities between a transcendent divinity and a finite human prevail over their similarities could help us to speak about God's nature and attributes in a more adequate way.

6.3 The Notion of Resistance and Its Potential Pitfalls

At first glance, it seems obvious that to be able to personally relate to God you cannot be resistant to such personal relationship. But is that right? Perhaps it is possible to personally relate to another person even while being resistant toward that person. If resistance comes in degrees, it might be the case that at least weak resistance does not make it impossible to enter a personal relationship with someone. Moreover, what if resistance toward personally relating to God is not only a conscious but also an unconscious disposition? If the latter is not implausible, how can we determine whether a person is resistant due to an unconscious disposition? What reasonable measures might there be for discerning whether self-deception may be involved? I find it somewhat problematic that Schellenberg does not give more attention to the concept of resistance since it plays an important role in his argument, especially in premise (7), where the lack of such resistance in at least one human being is claimed as an empirical fact and, when taken together with premises (4) and (6), entails that there is no God (see section 3).

6.4 Belief Is neither Indispensable nor Utterly Involuntary

I wonder why Schellenberg offers no argument for the claim that belief is a necessary condition for personal relationship with another person, but simply states it as a logical fact (see again, more recently, Schellenberg, 2019a: 103–104). This seems to suggest that, according to Schellenberg, those who deny the truth of this claim are not just factually wrong; they hold illogical views and deny a self-evident truth. But I think that the arguments by those who defend accounts of beliefless faith do not deserve this assessment. Additionally, I think there is a question which has not yet been satisfactorily answered as to exactly what the religious experience provided by sufficient experiential evidence for God's existence looks like, according to Schellenberg.

In my view, Schellenberg underestimates this renowned phenomenon of religious experience in the philosophy of religion (including in Schellenberg, 2019a: 101), especially compared with the attention this topic of religious experience is given, for example, by Rea (2018: 90–136). In regard to Schellenberg's claim that we have no control over our belief-forming habits, nor about what we believe or do not believe, I agree with Jackson and others that we may at least have direct control over our belief formation. That is, through direct control over our belief-forming habits we seem to have an impact on what evidence is available to us, and thus we have some indirect control over what we do or do not believe. As Schellenberg himself admits regarding what he presents as agnostic religion (i.e. a religion not built upon beliefs regarding its religious propositions), by "living a religious life one might gain access to relevant facts, for example through special experiences elicited by religious practice or special insights yielded by its concentrated attention on spiritual things" (Schellenberg, 2019b: 112).

6.5 Plausible Reasons for God to Allow Doubts about His Existence

The second reason why I do not think that the hiddenness argument succeeds in lowering the confidence in theism is that, as stated in section 4, there are promising defenses as to why God allows propositional hiddenness to occur. Due to space constraints, I am not able to defend my view that the objections against these defenses, by Schellenberg and others, do not succeed. I leave this task to another occasion.

7 Conclusion

Schellenberg's verdict is that "we have to conclude that the actual world is not the product of perfect love: no perfectly loving God exists" (Schellenberg,

2015a: 88). I hope that I have made a plausible case that there is still room for further reflection and debate, especially about the doctrine of God. That said, the concept of God Schellenberg endorses in his hiddenness argument is common in contemporary analytic debates. It seems reasonable when Schellenberg states that

> if you choose the category of a person to use when thinking about the divine, you should live with the results instead of backing off into skepticism suggesting that you haven't chosen any category at all. Of course, it's entirely possible to say much less about the divine – for example, you might say that there is some transcendent reality without putting any more into the description than that. But contemporary philosophical theists don't do this. They have proposed a personal divine. They should have the courage of their categories. (Schellenberg, 2019a: 150)

But the question is whether current philosophy of religion and theology should be obliged to adopt this specific understanding of theism – that of personal perfect being theism, or what Klaas Kraay labels "restricted theism" (Kraay, 2013: 257). After all, the hiddenness argument, if successful, helps us see the deficiencies of personal perfect being theism. As it is claimed regarding the argument from evil, "some people say that nonbelief provides evidence against theism only if we conceive of God in certain ways, and so we should conceive of God differently" (Howard-Snyder and Green, 2016).

What might we discover if all those engaged in the hiddenness debate were "open to learning from anything, anywhere" (Schellenberg, 2019b: 121), even regarding alternative theistic concepts of God?

References

Aijaz, Imran, and Markus Weidler (2007). Some critical reflections on the hiddenness argument. *International Journal for Philosophy of Religion* 61 (1): 1–23.

Anderson, Charity (2019). J. L. Schellenberg – *The hiddenness argument: Philosophy's new challenge to belief in God* (Oxford University Press, 2017). *International Journal for Philosophy of Religion* 86 (1): 85–89.

Andrews, Miles (2014). Divine hiddenness and affective forecasting. *Res Cogitans* 5 (1): 102–110.

Anselm of Canterbury (1968). Proslogion. In F. S. Schmitt, ed., *Opera Omnia*. Vol. 1. Stuttgart-Bad Cannstatt: Friedrich Frommann Verlag.

Aquinas, Thomas (1952). *Summa theologiae*. Vol. 1. Ed. by P. Caramello. Turin: Marietti.

Azadegan, Ebrahim (2014). Divine love and the argument from divine hiddenness. *European Journal for Philosophy of Religion* 6 (2): 101–116.

Baker-Hytch, Max (2016). Mutual epistemic dependence and the demographic divine hiddenness problem. *Religious Studies* 52 (3): 375–394.

Blanchard, Joshua (2016). Heschel, hiddenness, and the God of Israel. *European Journal for Philosophy of Religion* 8 (4): 109–124.

Buckareff, Andrei A., and Yujin Nagasawa (2016). Introduction: Alternative conceptions of divinity and contemporary analytic philosophy of religion. In A. A. Buckareff and Y. Nagasawa, eds., *Alternative Concepts of God: Essays on the Metaphysics of the Divine*. New York: Oxford University Press, 1–18.

Coakley, Sarah (2015). Divine hiddenness or dark intimacy? How John of the Cross dissolves a contemporary philosophical dilemma. In A. Green and E. Stump, eds., *Hidden Divinity and Religious Belief: New Perspectives*. New York: Cambridge University Press, 229–245.

Cockayne, Joshua (2018). The dark knight of the soul: Weaning and the problem of divine withdrawal. *Religious Studies* 54 (1): 73–90.

Crummett, Dustin (2015). "We are here to help each other": Religious community, divine hiddenness, and the responsibility argument. *Faith and Philosophy* 32 (1): 45–62.

Cruz, Helen de (2015). Divine hiddenness and the cognitive science of religion. In A. Green and E. Stump, eds., *Hidden Divinity and Religious Belief: New Perspectives*. New York: Cambridge University Press, 53–68.

Cruz, San Juan de la (1993). Noche oscura. In J. V. Rodríguez and F. R. Salvador, eds., *Obras Completas*. 5th critical ed. Madrid: Editorial de Espiritualidad, 431–487.

Cullison, Andrew (2010). Two solutions to the problem of divine hiddenness. *American Philosophical Quarterly* 47 (2): 119–134.

Cuneo, Terence (2013). Another look at divine hiddenness. *Religious Studies* 49 (2): 151–164 (Special Issue: Critical Essays on J. L. Schellenberg's Philosophy of Religion).

Davies, Brian (2004). *An Introduction to the Philosophy of Religion.* 3rd ed. New York: Oxford University Press.

Deng, Natalja (2019). *God and Time.* Cambridge, UK: Cambridge University Press.

Dougherty, Trent (2016). Reflections on the deep connection between problems of evil and problems of divine hiddenness. *European Journal for Philosophy of Religion* 8 (4): 65–84.

Drange, Theodore M. (1993). The argument from non-belief. *Religious Studies* 29 (4): 417–432.

Drange, Theodore M. (1998). *Nonbelief & Evil: Two Arguments for the Nonexistence of God.* Amherst, NY: Prometheus Books.

Dumsday, Travis (2010). Divine hiddenness and the responsibility argument: Assessing Schellenberg's argument against theism. *Philosophia Christi* 12 (2): 357–371.

Dumsday, Travis (2014). Divine hiddenness and the opiate of the people. *International Journal for Philosophy of Religion* 76 (2): 193–207.

Dierse, Ulrich, Wenzel Lohff, and Gunter Scholtz (2017). Offenbarung. In J. Ritter, K. Gründer, and G. Gabriel, eds., *Historisches Wörterbuch der Philosophie online.* https://doi.org//10.24894/HWPh.5315.

Evans, C. Stephen (2006). Can God be hidden and evident at the same time? Some Kierkegaardian reflections. *Faith and Philosophy* 23 (3): 241–253.

Fakhri, Omar (2020). The ineffability of God. *International Journal for the Philosophy of Religion.* https://doi.org/10.1007/s11153-020-09762-y.

Fales, Evan (2015). Journeying in perplexity. In A. Green and E. Stump, eds., *Hidden Divinity and Religious Belief: New Perspectives.* New York: Cambridge University Press, 89–105.

Fromm, Erich (1956). *The Art of Loving: An Enquiry into the Nature of Love.* New York: Harper & Row.

Greco, John (2015). No-fault atheism. In A. Green and E. Stump, eds., *Hidden Divinity and Religious Belief: New Perspectives.* New York: Cambridge University Press, 109–125.

Green, Adam, and Eleonore Stump, eds., (2015). *Hidden Divinity and Religious Belief: New Perspectives.* New York: Cambridge University Press.

Hendricks, Perry, and Kirk Lougheed (2019). Undermining the axiological solution to divine hiddenness. *International Journal for Philosophy of Religion* 86 (1): 3–15.

Henry, Douglas V. (2001). Does reasonable nonbelief exist? *Faith and Philosophy* 18 (1): 75–92.

Henry, Douglas V. (2008). Reasonable doubts about reasonable nonbelief. *Faith and Philosophy* 25 (3): 276–289.

Hick, John (1993). *God and the Universe of Faiths: Essays in the Philosophy of Religion.* London: The Macmillan Press.

Hick, John (2009). *Faith and Knowledge.* 2nd ed. Eugene, OR: Wipf and Stock.

Howard-Snyder, Daniel (1996). The argument from divine hiddenness. *Canadian Journal of Philosophy* 26 (3): 433–453.

Howard-Snyder, Daniel (2006). Hiddenness of God. In D. M. Borchert, ed., *Encyclopedia of Philosophy.* 2nd ed. Detroit, MI: Thomson Gale, 352–357.

Howard-Snyder, Daniel (2015). Divine openness and creaturely nonresistant nonbelief. In A. Green and E. Stump, eds., *Hidden Divinity and Religious Belief: New Perspectives.* New York: Cambridge University Press, 126–138.

Howard-Snyder, Daniel (2016). Does faith entail belief? *Faith and Philosophy* 33 (2): 142–162.

Howard-Snyder, Daniel, and Adam Green (2016). Hiddenness of God. In E. N. Zalta, ed., *Stanford Encyclopedia of Philosophy* (first published April 23, 2016). https://plato.stanford.edu/entries/divine-hiddenness.

Howard-Snyder, Daniel, and Adam Green (2017). *Dynamic Bibliography on Divine Hiddenness.* http://faculty.wwu.edu/~howardd/Bibliography%20on%20Divine%20Hiddenness.pdf.

Inwagen, Peter van (2006). *The Problem of Evil: The Gifford Lectures Delivered in the University of St. Andrews in 2003.* New York: Oxford University Press.

Jackson, Elizabeth (2016). Wagering against divine hiddenness. *European Journal for Philosophy of Religion* 8 (4): 85–108.

Kahane, Guy (2011). Should we want God to exist? *Philosophy and Phenomenological Research* 82 (3): 674–696.

Kraay, Klaas J. (2013). Method and madness in contemporary analytic philosophy of religion. *Toronto Journal of Theology* 29 (2): 245–264.

Kvanvig, Jonathan L (2002). Divine hiddenness: What is the problem? In D. Howard-Snyder and P. K. Moser, eds., *Divine Hiddenness: New Essays.* New York: Cambridge University Press, 149–163.

Lehe, Robert T. (2004). A response to the argument from the reasonableness of nonbelief. *Faith and Philosophy* 21 (2): 159–174.

References 47

Lougheed, Kirk (2018). The axiological solution to divine hiddenness. *Ratio* 31 (3): 331–341.

Lovering, Robert P. (2004). Divine hiddenness and inculpable ignorance. *International Journal for Philosophy of Religion* 56 (2): 89–107.

Maitzen, Stephen (2006). Divine hiddenness and the demographics of theism. *Religious Studies* 42 (2): 177–191.

Maitzen, Stephen (2008). Does Molinism explain the demographics of theism? *Religious Studies* 44 (4): 473–477.

Marsh, Jason (2008). Do the demographics of theistic belief disconfirm theism? A reply to Maitzen. *Religious Studies* 44 (4): 465–471.

Marsh, Jason (2013). Darwin and the problem of natural nonbelief. *The Monist* 96 (3): 349–376.

Mawson, Timothy J. (2012). The rationality of classical theism and its demographics. In Yujin Nagasawa, ed., *Scientific Approaches to the Philosophy of Religion*. London: Palgrave Macmillan, 184–204.

May, Rollo (1969). *Love and Will*. New York: W. W. Norton & Company.

McBrayer, Justin P., and Philip Swenson (2012). Scepticism about the argument from divine hiddenness. *Religious Studies* 48 (2): 129–150.

McGinnis, Jon (2015). The hiddenness of "divine hiddenness": Divine love in medieval Islamic lands. In A. Green and E. Stump, eds., *Hidden Divinity and Religious Belief: New Perspectives*. New York: Cambridge University Press, 157–174.

McKaughan, Daniel J. (2013). Authentic faith and acknowledged risk: Dissolving the problem of faith and reason. *Religious Studies* 49 (1): 101–124.

McKim, Robert (2001). *Religious Ambiguity and Religious Diversity*. New York: Oxford University Press.

Moser, Paul K. (2002). Cognitive idolatry and divine hiding. In D. Howard-Snyder and P. K. Moser, eds., *Divine Hiddenness: New Essays*. New York: Cambridge University Press, 120–148.

Moser, Paul K. (2015). Divine hiddenness and self-sacrifice. In A. Green and E. Stump, eds., *Hidden Divinity and Religious Belief: New Perspectives*. New York: Cambridge University Press, 71–88.

Murray, Michael J. (1993). Coercion and the hiddenness of God. *American Philosophical Quarterly* 30 (1): 27–38.

Murray, Michael J. (2002). Deus absconditus. In D. Howard-Snyder and P. K. Moser, eds., *Divine Hiddenness: New Essays*. New York: Cambridge University Press, 62–82.

Murray, Michael J., and David F. Dudrick (1995). Are coerced acts free? *American Philosophical Quarterly* 32 (2): 109–123.

Muyskens, James L. (1979). *The Sufficiency of Hope: The Conceptual Foundations of Religion*. Philadelphia, PA: Temple University Press.

Nagasawa, Yujin (2017). *Maximal God: A New Defence of Perfect Being Theism*. New York: Oxford University Press.

Oord, Thomas J. (2010). *Defining Love: A Philosophical, Scientific, and Theological Engagement*. Grand Rapids, MI: Brazos Press.

Perlmutter, Julian (2016). Desiring the hidden God: Knowledge without belief. *European Journal for Philosophy of Religion* 8 (4): 51–64.

Plantinga, Alvin (1974). *The Nature of Necessity*. New York: Oxford University Press.

Plantinga, Alvin (2000). *Warranted Christian Belief*. New York: Oxford University Press.

Price, H. H. (1965). Belief 'in' and belief 'that.' *Religious Studies* 1 (1): 5–27.

Rahner, Karl (1975). Über die Verborgenheit Gottes. In K. H. Neufeld, ed., *Schriften zur Theologie*. Vol.12. Zürich: Benziger Verlag Einsiedeln, 285–305.

Rea, Michael C. (2015). Hiddenness and transcendence. In A. Green and E. Stump, eds., *Hidden Divinity and Religious Belief: New Perspectives*. New York: Cambridge University Press, 210–225.

Rea, Michael C. (2018). *The Hiddenness of God*. New York: Oxford University Press.

Ross, Jacob Joshua (2002). The hiddenness of God: A puzzle or a real problem? In D. Howard-Snyder and P. K. Moser, eds., *Divine Hiddenness: New Essays*. New York: Cambridge University Press, 181–196.

Schärtl, Thomas (2016). Introduction: Rethinking the concept of a personal God. In T. Schärtl, C. Tapp, and V. Wegener, eds., *Rethinking the Concept of a Personal God: Classical Theism, Personal Theism, and Alternative Concepts of God*. Münster: Aschendorff Verlag, 3–31.

Schellenberg, John (1993). *Divine Hiddenness and Human Reason*. Ithaca, NY: Cornell University Press.

Schellenberg, J. L. (2002). What the hiddenness of God reveals: A collaborative discussion. In D. Howard-Snyder and P. K. Moser, eds., *Divine Hiddenness: New Essays*. New York: Cambridge University Press, 33–61.

Schellenberg, J. L. (2005a). The hiddenness argument revisited (I). *Religious Studies* 41 (2): 201–215.

Schellenberg, J. L. (2005b). The hiddenness argument revisited (II). *Religious Studies* 41 (3): 287–303.

Schellenberg, J. L. (2007). *The Wisdom to Doubt: A Justification of Religious Skepticism*. Ithaca, NY: Cornell University Press.

Schellenberg, J. L. (2008). Response to Tucker on hiddenness. *Religious Studies* 44 (3): 289–293.

Schellenberg, J. L. (2009). *The Will to Imagine: A Justification of Skeptical Religion*. Ithaca, NY: Cornell University Press.

Schellenberg, J. L. (2013). *Evolutionary Religion*. Oxford: Oxford University Press.

Schellenberg, J. L. (2015a). *The Hiddenness Argument: Philosophy's New Challenge to Belief in God*. New York: Oxford University Press.

Schellenberg, J. L. (2015b). Divine hiddenness and human philosophy. In A. Green and E. Stump, eds., *Hidden Divinity and Religious Belief: New Perspectives*. New York: Cambridge University Press, 13–32.

Schellenberg, J. L. (2017a). Divine hiddenness: Part 1 (recent work on the hiddenness argument). *Philosophy Compass* 12 (4): 1–9. https://doi.org/10.1111/phc3.12355.

Schellenberg, J. L. (2017b). Divine hiddenness: Part 2 (recent enlargements of the discussion). *Philosophy Compass* 12 (4): 1–10. https://doi.org/10.1111/phc3.12413.

Schellenberg, J. L. (2017c). Evil, hiddenness, and atheism. In P. K. Moser and C. Meister, eds., *The Cambridge Companion to the Problem of Evil*. New York: Cambridge University Press, 108–123.

Schellenberg, J. L. (2018). Triple transcendence, the value of God's existence, and a new route to atheism. In K. J. Kraay, ed., *Does God Matter? Essays on the Axiological Consequences of Theism*. New York: Routledge, 181–191.

Schellenberg, J. L. (2019a). *Progressive Atheism: How Moral Evolution Changes the God Debate*. New York: Bloomsbury Academic.

Schellenberg, J. L. (2019b). *Religion after Science: The Cultural Consequences of Religious Immaturity*. New York: Cambridge University Press.

Scott, Michael, and Gabriel Citron (2016). What is apophaticism? Ways of talking about an ineffable God. *European Journal for Philosophy of Religion* 8 (4): 23–49.

Swinburne, Richard (1979). *The Existence of God*. New York: Oxford University Press.

Swinburne, Richard (1998). *Providence and the Problem of Evil*. New York: Oxford University Press.

Swinburne, Richard (2004). *The Existence of God*. 2nd ed. New York: Oxford University Press.

Teeninga, Luke (2017). Divine hiddenness, greater goods, and accommodation. *Sophia* 56 (4): 589–603.

Trakakis, Nick (2007). An epistemically distant God? A critique of John Hick's response to the problem of divine hiddenness. *Heythrop Journal* 48 (2): 214–226.

Trakakis, N. N. (2015). The hidden divinity and what it reveals. In A. Green and E. Stump, eds., *Hidden Divinity and Religious Belief: New Perspectives*. New York: Cambridge University Press, 192–209.

Tucker, Chris (2008). Divine hiddenness and the value of divine–creature relationships. *Religious Studies* 44 (3): 269–287.

Vandergriff, Kevin. (2016). Natural nonbelief as a necessary means to a life of choiceworthy meaning. *Open Theology* 2 (1): 34–52.

Wainwright, William J. (2002). Jonathan Edwards and the hiddenness of God. In D. Howard-Snyder and P. K. Moser, eds., *Divine Hiddenness: New Essays*. New York: Cambridge University Press, 98–119.

Weidner, Veronika (2018). *Examining Schellenberg's Hiddenness Argument*. Cham, Switzerland: Palgrave Macmillan.

Wielenberg, Erik J. (2005). *Value and Virtue in a Godless Universe*. New York: Cambridge University Press.

Yandell, Keith E. (2012). *The Wisdom to Doubt: A Justification of Religious Skepticism*, by J. L. Schellenberg (Ithaca, NY: Cornell University Press, 2007), and *The Elusive God: Reorienting Religious Epistemology*, by Paul K. Moser (London: Cambridge University Press, 2009). *Mind* 121 (481): 205–217.

Cambridge Elements ☰

Philosophy of Religion

Yujin Nagasawa
University of Birmingham

Yujin Nagasawa is Professor of Philosophy and Co-Director of the John Hick Centre for Philosophy of Religion at the University of Birmingham. He is currently President of the British Society for the Philosophy of Religion. He is a member of the Editorial Board of *Religious Studies*, the *International Journal for Philosophy of Religion* and *Philosophy Compass*.

About the Series

This Cambridge Elements series provides concise and structured introductions to all the central topics in the philosophy of religion. It offers balanced, comprehensive coverage of multiple perspectives in the philosophy of religion. Contributors to the series are cutting-edge researchers who approach central issues in the philosophy of religion. Each provides a reliable resource for academic readers and develops new ideas and arguments from a unique viewpoint.

Cambridge Elements ≡

Philosophy of Religion

Elements in the Series

A full series listing is available at: www.cambridge.org/EPREL

Printed in the United States
by Baker & Taylor Publisher Services